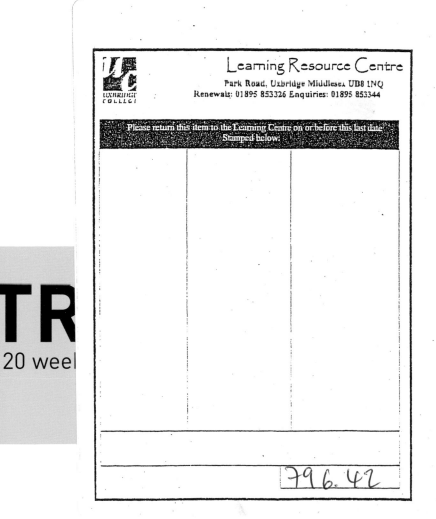

**TR**

20 week

rfield

# TRIATHLON

20 weeks to success in 5 hours a week

## mark barfield

A&C BLACK, LONDON

**FOR BRUCE AND SUE**

First published 2008
A&C Black Publishers Ltd
38 Soho Square
London W1D 3HB
www.acblack.com

The author acknowledges the British Triathlon Federation Coach Education Department for the use of some formats used in this publication.

Photo on p.155 © Gerard Brown
All other photos © Nigel Farrow

ISBN 978-1-408-10009-7

A CIP catalogue record for this book is available from the British Library.

This book is produced using paper from wood grown in managed, sustainable forests. It is natural, renewable and recyclable. The logging and manufacturing processes conform to the environmental regulations of the country of origin.

Typeset in New Baskerville by Palimpsest Book Production Limited,
Grangemouth, Stirlingshire

Printed and bound in China

# CONTENTS

# FOREWORD

Why is triathlon acknowledged today as the fastest growing sport in Great Britain and elsewhere in the world?

Because of the attraction of discovering how to stretch the boundaries beyond the challenges of our daily life and to have a few boasting rights at home, in the office and amongst our friends, and to say 'I am a triathlete!'

Because triathlon can be tailored to suit everyone's desires, with a race or training opportunity for everyone.

Because triathlon can offer all ages, from youngster to octogenarian, a fantastic multi-sport experience through welcoming clubs, all over the country, offering the novice a safe and stable environment to learn, train and improve, including clubs especially accredited for kids and disabled athletes too.

Because it is a sport at the cutting edge of technology: kit and clothing options are awesome!

Because we can all compete alongside modest, elite Olympians too, creating a camaraderie, joie de vivre and passion for the sport that is unique.

Because that delicious, nervous tingle of anticipation, excitement, and a little fear, as the starting claxon signals the melee of a swim, transforms into fierce determination to succeed throughout the disciplines and much exhilaration at reaching the finish line.

Because the habit of triathlon training is catching, it is great fun, and can change your life if you want it to – it did mine!

British Triathlon (BTF) is now 25 years old and governs nationally, what is now a summer Olympic sport. Many of the Board of Directors, staff, coaches, officials and volunteers have been members since the beginning, and are still contributing today, to attract others to join in. Please come and join us.

**Dr Sarah Springman**
**President, British Triathlon Federation**

*Sarah Springman has been a successful elite triathlete and duathlete, is a BTF Level 2 coach and still participates as an age grouper today, a quarter of a century after she did her first novice triathlon. She was even champion in her age category in the World Winter Triathlon in 2006! She became BTF President in 2007 and was awarded the OBE for services to sport in 1997.*

**The modern triathlon is an endurance sport, over various distances, comprising three disciplines – running, swimming and cycling. Each sport is run back-to-back and the shortest time taken to complete all these disciplines, including 'transitions', decides the winner.**

## WHAT IS A TRIATHLON?

Triathlon is now the biggest event that we refer to as 'multi-sport', a concept that is developing into a number of subtly different forms including duathlon (run, bike, run) and aquathlon (swim, run). Triathlon is at the heart of most of these forms and remains the inspiration for developments of format, distance and compilation.

The triathlon season is traditionally restricted to the summer months, though this is extended by duathlon (run, cycle, run) and aquathlon (swim, run): these events are used by developing and club athletes to prepare for and wind down from the racing season. There are also winter events, but these typically include cross-country skiing or ice speed skating as part of their make-up.

Triathlon is often referred to as the fastest growing Olympic sport and has developed a very strong following across the world. The number of events, clubs and athletes increases every year, as does the profile of the sport as media coverage increases. There are races of different distances that allow individuals of all abilities to start this exciting and challenging sport, and to progress to compete in races

of Olympic distance or even to progress to the long-distance events called Ironman.

Triathlon has an interesting history that started in the UK in the early 1980s with three athletes, a swimmer, a cyclist and a runner, arguing over who was the best athlete. The challenge was set for an event that combined the three and so the triathlon was born. Largely in a long-distance format, triathlon has developed into races of all distances and it became an Olympic sport in Sydney in 2000. The sport of triathlon has many unique aspects including the opportunity for all athletes of all ages to compete in national, European and world championships. This is made possible by an age group system that puts all athletes into five-year age groups for competition. This aspect of the sport is often attractive as it gives a clear pathway for progression for talented athletes at all levels. The other, more obvious, unique aspect of triathlon is the continuous nature of the events. The clock is running from the start of the swim through to the completion of the run. This means that you are timed getting out of the pool, onto the bike and then again when moving from bike to run. This includes the time taken to change clothing, footwear and safety equipment and this element comprises what is often referred to as the fourth discipline of triathlon. For elite athletes this element can be the difference between winning or losing. For the recreational athlete the challenge is a little different but no less taxing.

Triathlons are run at all sorts of venues from the famous Hawaii Ironman triathlon to the local swimming pool-based event we will be focusing on in this book. Open water swimming is a staple part of the seasoned triathlete's competitive season, though nearly all athletes will have started their triathlon career with a swimming pool-based event and this kind of event will provide necessary experience without the added complication of swimming in the sea or a lake.

# UNDERSTANDING DUATHLON AND AQUATHLON

Triathlon is a multi-sport event and is part of a family of events that have developed alongside triathlon. The two most prominent within this family are duathlon and aquathlon. There are national, European and world championships in both these events.

Duathlon comprises a running section and a cycling section followed by a second run. Clearly if you are an accomplished runner this event will suit you. The nature of the start of this event also appeals to people, as the first run is normally a mass start shoulder-to-shoulder run which allows for a different type of competitive feeling, as opposed to the starts in smaller groups or as an individual that will be experienced in most novice triathlons. This kind of start can be a little daunting as some pushing and shoving may well take place (although this breaks the rules), but you will get the feeling of competing against others straight away. Duathlons are run throughout the year but are more common at the beginning and end of the racing season (when you may not want to be outside after a swim).

There are also a number of mid-week racing series that allow people to compete during the week rather than just at the weekend. Duathlons do have standard distances, as in triathlon, but there is a variety of the race distances available.

An aquathlon is a simple swim and run event, often beginning with a mass start: the first runner over the line wins. In the summer there are a number of open water series that are great for giving people the experience of racing in open water. At the beginning and end of the season there are also some pool-based aquathlons which have a different starting process, normally with very small groups of athletes or, more frequently, individual athletes starting one at a time.

There are other variations on the triathlon theme. Many gyms now run indoor triathlons. These normally use a rowing machine, a cycling machine and a running machine with a set distance on all three. The total time for all three is calculated; some even include the transition time between machines. There is also off-road triathlon which, as the name suggests, is run off-road with a cross-country style run and a cross-country mountain bike race. This obviously requires some additional skills and equipment but it is a good extension of the sport.

Many people's first impressions of triathlon are based on the long-distance epic races, such as the Ironman Hawaii, which can often be a little off-putting. This book will show you that with a little commitment and guidance you can tackle a much more accessible sprint or super sprint distance triathlon. This means a race of the following distances:

Swim    400–750m
Bike    10–20km
Run    3–5km.

At first sight these distances may appear a little daunting, but by following the training programme outlined in this book you will progress from someone who has an aspiration to an athlete with ability. This book will not make you a world champion but, as you will see from our case study, there are many athletes who have started triathlon later in life and have gone on to represent their countries as international athletes. That ambition can be at the back of your mind but first of all we need to get you both to the start line and then successfully to the finish line of your first triathlon. It is on this that we will focus in this book.

Many people are put off triathlon and other endurance sports because they feel they don't have the time to develop the skills and fitness necessary for them to take part. We will show that by assigning a regular weekly set of training sessions and by organising your life you can become a triathlete. Most people have to fit training for sport around work, family, life and other commitments and it is for these people that we have written this book. By following this

programme you will feel healthier, be fitter and have developed a new hobby; you will probably sleep a lot better, too, and start to feel like an athlete.

We will discuss finding the right event for you as well as talking about how to get started and the equipment you will need. We will then take you through a week-by-week programme to guide you from your starting point to race day. You are unlikely to get through this programme without problems, either an irritating cold or infection or a change in circumstances at home or work that may temporarily interrupt your training: this is inevitable at some point but

should not cause any panic. You should simply resume training when you can and not try to catch up with missed sessions.

When selecting an event give yourself as much time as possible. While this book is titled '20 weeks to success in five hours a week', a longer period of preparation will give you more time to cope with the little challenges that life throws at us such as illness, holidays, celebrations and work interruptions.

## SELECTING AN EVENT

The first step of any journey is always the most difficult. In the case of triathlon there is a degree of planning that needs to be done to ensure that you can compete in the event. As a challenge a triathlon is unique yet achievable. A basic level of fitness is required but any relatively healthy person can prepare for and complete a sprint or super sprint distance triathlon we are aiming for in this book. As we mentioned, triathlons are run over a variety of recognised distances:

- Super sprint triathlons: swim of 400m, cycle of 10km and a run of 2.5km.
- Sprint triathlons: swim of 750m, a cycle of 20km and a run of 5km.
- Standard distance triathlons: swim of 1500m, a cycle of 40km and a run of 10km.
- Long distance or Ironman: swim of 3000m, a cycle of 120km and a run of 30km.

# IRONMAN – THE LEGEND OF KONA

Held in October every year, the Kona Ironman Triathlon is now the Ironman world championships. As with all triathlons, this event encompasses three major endurance events on the island. These events are the 3.86 kilometre ocean swim in Kailua Kona Bay, the 180.2 kilometre bike race across the Hawaiian lava desert to Hawi and back and concluding with the marathon run (26.2 kilometres) across the island. This event has now developed into one of the biggest triathlons in the world and places on the starting line are much coveted in the triathlon community. Most places in this event, which is the father of all triathlons, are achieved through high finishing places in Ironman races across the world during the previous year. Ironman itself is a brand owned by the World Triathlon Corporation. Ironman races are organised across the world and are often oversubscribed. Ironman itself is a recognised brand.

The focus of this book will be on the super and sprint distance events but you will find many events that don't strictly follow the distances. For the purposes of this book we will be preparing for events that are between 400 and 750 metres of swimming, 10 and 20 kilometres of cycling and 2.5 and 5 kilometres of running. If you are confident of your ability to cover these distances then aim for the longer distance event; if you are not so confident or you have less experience in any of the three disciplines then target the shorter distance. If you are entering a local race the distances may be set, and providing they are not considerably longer than those detailed above the programme will be sufficient. If the distances are much longer, approaching standard race distance, then you will probably need to enter a shorter sprint or super sprint race first; the programme in this book will be appropriate for the training aimed at the shorter race.

Sprint and super sprint triathlons are very popular and relatively common as they are easier to organise and run than longer triathlons. Finding an event should not be too difficult but a degree of planning will be required to ensure you identify a suitable event and get a place. This is especially important for the more popular events and in the spring when shorter races are particularly popular with seasoned athletes building up to a full season of triathlon. There are also now world championships over the sprint distance and you may find some shorter races being used as qualifying events.

Triathlon events are normally well presented on the internet with many clubs and commercial organisers having websites to promote their events, many offering online entry systems. Larger newsagents usually carry some form of triathlon magazine and this will be full of race information both in the events listings and in advertisements for the events themselves in the sprint and super sprint category. You should think about the type of experience you want. Many triathlon clubs organise small local events that are very friendly and well run, but there are also larger commercial organisers that run larger events with a more comprehensive infrastructure that will be more expensive but may give you the feeling of being part of a bigger, more

exciting event. You may also need to consider which part of the country you want to race in. Local support from family and friends may be a consideration and should not be underestimated as a morale booster during the later stages of the event, but you may wish to consider taking part in a race in a particularly attractive part of the country or at a venue you find appealing. This can give an added incentive and can allow you to build a weekend around the event to add to the feeling of working towards a larger goal.

## Other considerations when selecting an event

Events do differ in style. The sprint or super sprint race we are considering will mainly be pool-based events: as a first triathlon it is this style of event that you should focus on. Open water swimming is an aspect of triathlon that many find appealing but it does present some additional challenges to the novice. Firstly, it will almost certainly require a wetsuit, which is costly and it is not always easy to get one with a suitable fit for simply swimming. There are also additional techniques that must be learned and practised, which in the short time we have in this book would be tricky. The style of racing is also slightly different with swimmers setting off in larger groups. This is a little daunting for even the most seasoned of athletes and is not the best environment for a novice triathlete.

So, having narrowed our event selection to a pool-based swim there are a couple of other options to consider. You may find that in the early or later season there are events that are run and ridden entirely off-road. If you are not a confident rider on the open road then this may be something to consider, though you will almost certainly need a mountain bike and the course may be technically more challenging.

There are many events where the run is described as off-road. This may indicate a trail-based run on pathways or a run around the perimeter of a field, or it may be a cross-country style run through mud and challenging terrain. Depending on your preference you can make your choice and know what to expect, and train appropriately for it.

## THE AGE GROUP SYSTEM

One of the most exciting aspects of triathlon is the way in which people compete. If you enter a long-distance running race such as a marathon you will be given your time and position overall. In a triathlon you will get this information and also you will be able to see where you came against people of the same sex and age. This means that there is genuine competition for everyone and you

are always able to race people of a similar age and the same sex as you. This gives a realistic target if you wish to progress as a competitive triathlete and allows for regional competition at all levels. Almost all triathlons are run along these lines and there are competitions at all levels for athletes in every age group. This starts at a regional, and in some cases county level, and progresses through national championships to European and world championships. This means that at any age you can be a champion of your region, nation or, if you are good enough, the world. The age categories are applied in five-year bands as detailed below.

The following age categories will apply at British Triathlon registered events:

| Code | Category | Age |
|------|----------|-----|
| 8 | TriStar Start | 8 |
| 9–10 | TriStars 1 | 9–10 |
| 11–12 | TriStars 2 | 11–12 |
| 13–14 | TriStars 3 | 13–14 |
| A | Youths | 15–16 |
| B | Juniors 17–18 | 17–18 |
| C | Juniors 19 | 19 |
| D | Senior 1 | 20–24 |
| E | Senior 2 | 25–29 |
| F | Senior 3 | 30–34 |
| G | Senior 4 | 35–39 |
| H | Veteran 1 | 40–44 |
| I | Veteran 2 | 45–49 |
| J | Veteran 3 | 50–54 |
| K | Veteran 4 | 55–59 |
| L | Veteran 5 | 60–64 |
| M | Veteran 6 | 65–69 |
| N | Veteran 7 | 70–74 |
| P | Veteran 8 | 75–79 |
| Q | Veteran 9 | 80+ |

Age category is determined as at 31 December in the current year.

## RACE DOCUMENTATION AND APPLICATIONS

All events require an entry form of some description; some clubs and commercial organisers provide this online, while others will send entry forms and information by post. Your completed form will need to be accompanied by payment to secure your place in the race and usually a quick chat with the race organiser will help answer any queries you may have concerning the course and help you complete the form. These entry forms only require very straightforward information. You will be asked about club membership and whether you are a member of your national triathlon governing body, such as Triathlon England. This is to ensure that you are adequately insured when you take part. Triathlon England provides insurance for all its members and membership of the organisation proves to the race promoter that you are covered to race. If you are not a member of your national triathlon governing body you will be given the option to join for the day of the race, which will cover you for the duration of the event. You will be charged an additional fee on top of the race entry fee for this membership but the insurance is vital for all competitors. If

you find you enjoy triathlon and want to take part in more, full membership of your national triathlon governing body is recommended as you will also receive a handbook, a regular magazine and insurance cover for both racing and training as well as access to other membership benefits.

## FINAL PREPARATIONS FOR RACE DAY

There are a few things that need to be considered and planned before race day. Your race details should arrive within a couple of weeks of the event. With many organisers now having online entry, receipt of entries can be confirmed by e-mail, and sometimes a list of entrants will be displayed on their websites so you can be sure your entry has not gone missing. If you are in any way concerned then give the organiser a call, make sure they have your entry and ask for details about the race. This will help you plan the next bit.

Once you have entered your event there is nothing to worry about until a few weeks before the event, when you will receive joining instructions. You may find details of the course on the race website, if there is one – this will prove useful if you are focusing on an event that has a particular characteristic, such as a particularly hilly course or one that is susceptible to winds.

If the event is any distance from where you live you will need to think about travel and accommodation. Most triathlons start relatively early in the morning during the weekend which may mean a very early start or an overnight stay. If you are more than, say, ninety minutes from the race venue it is probably worth staying overnight as this will ensure you are better rested and haven't spent a great deal of time cramped in a car immediately before the race. Also some races require you to register in person the day before the race which will of course require either a great deal of travelling or an overnight stay. If you are travelling on the day of the event then consider your route carefully to make sure you arrive at the venue with plenty of time to spare. If you are staying overnight then think about where you will be staying well in advance: there are many athletes who can tell stories of roaring parties taking place in the hotel the night before an event, guaranteeing a disturbed night's sleep, so careful research can pay dividends when booking a place to stay. Also consider where, when and what you will be eating on the morning of the race. Many hotels have a much later breakfast at weekends and you may need to take your own food to ensure you get something suitable before the race.

Regardless of the conditions about registration times imposed by the organiser you should aim to arrive at the venue sixty to ninety minutes before your start time. This will allow you time to set up your transition area and complete a warm up as well as familiarising yourself with the layout of the transition and race routes before your start time. The last thing you want to do is be rushing and flustered in these last few important moments before you race.

Making sure you have all the right kit with you is vital. Take care when packing your bag with your clothing and where possible take a few extra bits. Most experienced triathletes seem to travel with at least three pairs of goggles as these seem to be the one piece of kit that will break the second you try to put them on before the race.

Take care when packing your bike for transportation. Regardless of your mode of transport, it is always worth taking your bike for a quick ride (with your helmet on) before you put it into the transition area to make sure that it has been put together correctly and is functioning as you need it to. There is often a bike retailer on site at events that can supply last-minute essentials but you should not rely on this; try to take everything that you think you will need, as well as some of the stuff you hope you won't such as spare inner tubes, etc.

## TRAINING WITH OTHERS

As a rapidly growing sport, triathlon has an infrastructure that is developing to support it. This extends beyond races into clubs. There are many clubs across the country which cater for triathletes of all abilities. This book is focused on allowing you to train alone and to

succeed but training with other people may be something that appeals to you. Triathlon clubs are usually friendly places but to some people they can be a little daunting. Understand that everyone was once a novice and has probably, in the history of a rather young sport, experienced many of the emotions that you are currently feeling. One of the key benefits of working with a triathlon club is the provision of triathlon coaches. Most good clubs will have coaches who can provide you with advice that, when combined with the programme in this book, will help you to progress to your goal. A coach can be especially useful when analysing and improving your swimming; there may be some minor errors in your swim stroke that can be easily solved and will have a huge impact on your swimming ability and efficiency.

Training with other people also has the additional benefit of motivation; working towards your goal with other people is often far more rewarding than doing it on your own. Clubs generally have a number of group training sessions during the week. These will probably be spread across a number of disciplines and will usually cover all abilities. Attending a group session will help you to develop your technique and the company of others will help you stick with things when you would rather be at home on the sofa. Training on a cold evening will appear much more interesting if you are working with other people.

If the triathlon club option does not appeal to you or you do not have a local club then consider training with a friend. Your training partner needs to be of a similar ability and have the same goal as you. By working with someone else you are much more likely to stick to the programme in this book. You will need to find mutually convenient training times, which may be more restrictive for you, but the overall effect of working with somebody else on a shared goal may be worth any personal inconvenience.

Identifying the opportunities you have to train, with a partner, club or on your own, is a vital part of working out not only how to train and what training to do, which is what this book is all about, but also, through a process of self-analysis, when you can train. The form below will enable you to look at your day on a week-by-week basis and identify your potential training opportunities. If these coincide with club sessions that you want to attend then great; if not, how will it be possible for you to change your day to accommodate the open club sessions?

## WEEKLY TRAINING SCHEDULE

|       | MON | TUE | WED | THUR | FRI | SAT | SUN |
|-------|-----|-----|-----|------|-----|-----|-----|
| 06.00 |     |     |     |      |     |     |     |
| 06.30 |     |     |     |      |     |     |     |
| 07.00 |     |     |     |      |     |     |     |
| 07.30 |     |     |     |      |     |     |     |
| 08.00 |     |     |     |      |     |     |     |
| 08.30 |     |     |     |      |     |     |     |
| 09.00 |     |     |     |      |     |     |     |
| 09.30 |     |     |     |      |     |     |     |
| 10.00 |     |     |     |      |     |     |     |
| 10.30 |     |     |     |      |     |     |     |
| 11.00 |     |     |     |      |     |     |     |
| 11.30 |     |     |     |      |     |     |     |
| 12.00 |     |     |     |      |     |     |     |
| 12.30 |     |     |     |      |     |     |     |
| 13.00 |     |     |     |      |     |     |     |
| 13.30 |     |     |     |      |     |     |     |
| 14.00 |     |     |     |      |     |     |     |
| 14.30 |     |     |     |      |     |     |     |
| 15.00 |     |     |     |      |     |     |     |
| 15.30 |     |     |     |      |     |     |     |
| 16.00 |     |     |     |      |     |     |     |
| 16.30 |     |     |     |      |     |     |     |
| 17.00 |     |     |     |      |     |     |     |
| 17.30 |     |     |     |      |     |     |     |
| 18.00 |     |     |     |      |     |     |     |
| 18.30 |     |     |     |      |     |     |     |
| 19.00 |     |     |     |      |     |     |     |
| 19.30 |     |     |     |      |     |     |     |
| 20.00 |     |     |     |      |     |     |     |
| 20.30 |     |     |     |      |     |     |     |
| 21.00 |     |     |     |      |     |     |     |

If you are working with a training partner you should both complete this schedule and then look for a mutually compatible time slot; this may require a degree of flexibility and compromise.

If you are a shift worker this may be more difficult and may require completing on a weekly basis to help you identify your five training slots. These training slots will be the

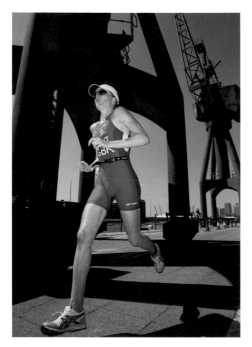

## 1

## IMPROVING YOUR FITNESS

Training for a triathlon is a fantastic thing to do. It will give you a real sense of achievement and your family and friends will be proud of you for working hard and finishing an event that is exciting and appealing. On top of this achievement you will be making a significant and possibly long-term change to your health, fitness and well-being. So, how can training for triathlon make you healthier and fitter?

Training for your triathlon will make you fitter. Fitness is measured in a number of different ways; probably the most important of these is an improvement in the function of the heart combined with efficient breathing. This cardiovascular function is how the body transports oxygen around the body. Muscles need oxygen to make them work and improvements in this component of fitness make everyday activities easier. This improvement will be gained by following the programme in this book, and as triathlon is predominantly a sport that requires cardiovascular ability the improvements in fitness will be most noticeable in this area. In your everyday life you will notice that you are able to walk up stairs without being out of breath and you will be able to walk for further without tiring. You will be able to walk, jog or run further and faster as your cardiovascular fitness improves. This will also apply to your swimming and cycling ability. You may even notice an improvement in your cardiovascular ability in other areas as well!

period that you are going to train during any given week: clearly this will be more difficult to identify if you are working a shift pattern, but the planning is vital to ensure that the training does take place. Every effort has been made to keep the training sessions in this book to a manageable length but as you become more experienced and as the book progresses you will find some of the sessions getting longer. Keep track of the estimated session length and don't forget to take into account any travelling and changing time.

Fitness is also measured by local muscular endurance – the ability to carry out a given action repeatedly. This is clearly a really important area for all three elements of the triathlon as there are repetitive actions required in swimming, cycling and running. Initially this can be a slightly painful part of the process of becoming a triathlete. For muscles to improve their ability to carry out these activities the process that you go through involves microscopic damage to muscle fibres. The body's response to this microscopic damage, which is inflicted through exercise, is not only to repair the damage but to also make sure that the damage is not as easily inflicted again by repairing the muscle fibres stronger than before. This process can cause a little muscular soreness and aches. This will be relatively short lived, normally no more than a day or so, and we will do our best to ensure that the progression of the training programme will be steady enough to prevent as many aches and pains as possible.

Fitness is also measured by muscular strength and you may find that your ability in certain areas will improve, but this is not something that we are specifically targeting in this book – our target is to achieve a triathlon finish, not become a body builder.

There are two other methods of measuring fitness: one relates to reaction times and the other relates to flexibility. Reaction times will improve as your cardiovascular fitness and local muscular endurance get better. In endurance events reaction times are a lot less critical than they are for team games and for this reason we will not be focusing on them in this book

On first inspection flexibility is not vitally important for triathlon. However, depending on your level of physical activity before starting the programme in this book it will be necessary to improve some areas of your flexibility to allow you to perform the physical movements required to swim, cycle and run. The other area in which improvements in flexibility will be beneficial is in injury prevention. By following a training programme and putting your body under a degree of stress, albeit in a very controlled way with a specific outcome, there is a risk of injury. These injuries may be prevented in many cases by ensuring that flexibility is maintained and developed. We will do this by completing stretching exercises at the end of every training session.

# STRETCHING

Use all the following stretches and hold them very still, without bouncing or forcing, for twenty to thirty seconds. Many people stretch as part of the warm-up process that we use at the beginning of every training session but we will not be using this, as it is commonly understood that it is not required unless you are carrying out activities that are explosive and this is not really required for triathlon. By performing these warm-down stretches you will also help prevent too many post-exercise aches and pains, ensuring you can continue with the training, as well as improving your overall flexibility.

Stretch one for calf muscles. This stretch works on the large muscle of the calves, which are made up of two muscle groups. Keeping your heels on the floor, lean in towards the wall until you feel a stretch in the centre of the fleshy part at the centre of the muscle. Place your hands on the wall to offer stability and hold the stretch very still. You may find your heel starting to creep up; very gently ease it back into position as you hold the stretch.

This is the second stretch for the lower part of the calf muscles. Staying in the same position against the wall, bring your leg towards the wall and move your weight onto the forward foot until you can feel a stretch in the lower part of the calf muscle just above your heel.

This is the stretch for the front of the thigh. Using the wall to balance, bring the heel of one leg up towards your bottom. Reach back and hold your foot around the ankle. Keep your knees together and push your hips forwards. The stretch should be felt in the middle of the thigh.

This is a stretch for the inner thigh. Sit on the floor, keep your back straight and bring your heels together. Slowly bring your heels in towards your body until you feel a stretch in the upper inner thigh.

This is stretch for the hamstring at the back of the leg. Sit on the floor with a straight back and extend one leg out straight, not to the side of your body, with your toes pointing straight up in the air. Relax your other leg into a comfortable position and lean forwards into the extended leg. The stretch should be felt in the centre of the upper part of the leg.

This stretch is for the buttocks and can be done standing up or lying on the floor. Bring your knee up towards your chest while keeping your back as straight as possible. Bring your knee slightly across your body towards the opposite elbow. The stretch should be felt in the centre of the buttock.

## OTHER HEALTH BENEFITS

Having outlined the benefits that training for your triathlon will have on your fitness, let's look at how this will make you more healthy. Weight loss is an obvious benefit. This book is definitely not a diet manual nor is weight loss a major target for what we are doing. However, the natural process of increasing your physical activity will burn more calories than you would normally do. This process will probably help you to reduce your weight. This weight loss, combined with the strengthening of the heart which is a by-product of the cardiovascular improvements we discussed earlier, will ensure that your health improves. The overall process of improved fitness and some possible weight loss have been linked to a reduced risk of high blood pressure, diabetes, heart disease, and even cancer.

As with weight loss, there are no guarantees that this training will prevent any of these conditions, though it is well documented that a gradual and continual exercise programme will improve your overall health, help you sleep better and improve your general well being.

You can improve your health and fitness by following this programme but the best effects will be gained by staying active and participating long-term in physical activity.

## ARE YOU HEALTHY ENOUGH TO START TRAINING?

To achieve these benefits and avoid any activity-related injuries or fatigue-related illness it is essential that you are in a reasonable condition to start training and if you have any concerns these must be resolved before your first week's training. The programme must be adhered to as closely as possible. It is really important that you do not train too hard or for too long at the early stages of the programme even though you may feel that you can tackle more. Sticking to the guidelines we give you will help prevent injury and ensure that you get to the start and finish line in great shape.

As a responsible publication we need to make sure that you are not putting yourself in danger by taking part in a training programme. This may sound a little dramatic but sedentary people must be careful when starting any activity programme. This process is exactly the same as if you were joining a gym; if you are already a member of a gym and have been exercising regularly for a while then this process is less important. Obviously we won't be able to weigh you or take your blood pressure so the responsibility must sit with you to ensure that you don't put yourself at risk. If in doubt, seek medical advice.

Even if you are a regular exerciser you still need to be cautious and listen very carefully to your body. This is a phrase that is used often but seldom explained. It is about understanding your response to exercise and activity. As we explained before, you may experience some aches and pains as you progress through the programme. You will very quickly learn where and how these effects are felt and any pains that are out of the ordinary need to be taken seriously. Pains that occur in the joints or chest must also be taken seriously and any sharp pains may also indicate problems that need medical attention.

The intervention of a doctor may seem extreme but it must be resorted to if you have any concerns. As a guide to pre-exercise screening there are a number of questions detailed below. If you answer yes to any of these questions it is advisable to contact a doctor:

- Have you sought medical advice for a heart condition?
- Do you experience chest pains?
- Do you have a bone or joint problem?
- Do you have low or high blood pressure?
- Are you pregnant?
- Are you a diabetic?
- Are you an asthmatic?
- Are you over 60 years of age?
- Have you had an injury in the last 6 months?
- Have you had a cold in the last 2 weeks?
- Do you know of any reason why you should not increase your physical activity?

Depending on your GP, you may find that you are charged for a pre-exercise medical. Many doctors will run through your concerns and advise you accordingly. However, most doctors are not experts in sport and exercise so they may not always be able to offer detailed advice.

If the advice is not to participate then you might want to consider a second opinion from a doctor with sports and exercise experience. If the advice is to start slowly then our programme should be suitable, though you may like to take some additional time to build up to the distances and endurances that we will be setting.

Starting your planning for a triathlon can be a little daunting but it is in this phase that you will get the most benefit from some careful consideration. You will be making some great changes to your lifestyle which will have a positive impact on your health; taking a little time early on to consider your current position is a sensible step that will help you be successful in the long run.

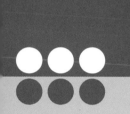

2

# swimming

## EQUIPMENT

Watching triathlon on the television you may be excused for thinking that your entry into the sport will be expensive. This does not have to be the case though you are going to have to think about what kit you will need to both get the most out of your training and, more importantly, to enjoy it in comfort. The best approach is to work through the disciplines and look at the equipment you will need.

Let's now look at the equipment you may need to race. Swimming is easily covered by the equipment listed elsewhere in the swimming chapter though you will need to remember that you will be cycling and running in your kit as well. You can get a triathlon-specific outfit for racing though this is an additional investment. There are a number of different types of triathlon clothing available.

A plastic box is ideal for carrying your equipment and storing everything in the transition area. It will also help you to recognise your spot in the transition area.

There are many equipment considerations for a sport which has three distinct parts.

Hopefully, a minimum of kit can get you started but the list of equipment you could buy is almost endless. Essentially you need some basic swim kit, some decent trainers and a bike. Anything else, with the exception of the helmet, is probably nice to have rather than vital; it really depends on your budget and your future aspirations when it comes to deciding how much equipment you invest in.

Your basic swimming costume needs to be a sports swimming costume. For men this means a close-fitting swim suit. The Bermuda shorts style of swimming outfit may be more flattering but the drag from the extra sodden material will slow you

down. If completion rather than speed is your main goal, the extra energy required to drag the material in a pair of long baggy shorts through the pool would be better used in the run and bike. A close fitting pair of standard swim trunks will also wash and dry better, making your post-training chores a bit less onerous. For women, a one-piece costume is probably best though there are many sport-specific, as opposed to leisure, two-piece costumes that are very good. Costumes that are designed for sport will provide support where required and will be less susceptible to movement caused by drag in the water, thereby protecting the modesty of the wearer. A large thin absorbent towel is probably best for drying after pool sessions. A smaller hand towel may also be a good idea for quickly drying your hair and/or your feet at the end of a session. Keeping all this in a bag with your other swimming kit is a good idea. The capacity of your holdall along with its ability to dry and fold up (to fit into lockers) should be a consideration.

Many people find that swimming with goggles not only makes the swim more pleasurable but also possibly faster and certainly more efficient. Regardless of your technique, goggles will protect your eyes from chlorine which is easily splashed even if you are using a swim style, stroke or technique which does not involve putting your face in the water. Choosing goggles can be a very personal matter but as a basic guideline use a sports shop, ask to try the goggles on, ensure that they have plenty of adjustment and are comfortable on your face in around the eye pieces and the nose bridge. Most goggles are anti-fog now and should be less susceptible to steaming up during your swim; this feature also makes your swim safer. Many swimmers have two pairs of goggles as they do seem to have a habit of getting lost or the elastic strap breaking without warning, though good care following a swim can help prevent this. Cost should not be a huge concern as even very good quality goggles are not terribly expensive. If you wear glasses some goggles can be fitted with your prescription, though these are obviously more expensive. Most triathlon magazines carry advertisements for such items in the classified sections or

your optician should be able to help. Goggles should be washed with clean lukewarm water after each session and checked for wear and tear.

Footwear may seem a strange item to include under swimming but there are many people who find the swimming experience is improved by wearing pool shoes when walking from the changing area to the pool. Wearing shoes can also help prevent picking up verrucas from the pool surfaces; these can be uncomfortable and have an impact on your running or cycling. Pool shoes or flip-flops can be bought very cheaply. Other equipment that you may want to add to your swimming bag includes shampoo, shower gel, comb/brush, deodorant, etc, carrier

# FOCUS ON THE EQUIPMENT OBSESSION

As with every sport where equipment is required there is an advantage, however small, to using cutting-edge equipment design. With triathlon there are three aspects to this and the opportunity to spend huge amounts of money are vast.

## The cutting edge of swimming

Swimwear company Speedo and other manufacturers are always trying to improve the streamline nature of their swimwear. Speedo and Orca have developed all-in-one bodysuits, the *Fastskin FSII* and *Pro Killa*.

## So how does it work?

The suit is designed to help the swimmer glide through the pool as efficiently as possible. Believe it or not, your body creates friction as you move through the water with friction varying across the body. This causes 'passive drag' – a tiny amount of resistance that means you don't move as smoothly as you may think.

## How was the suit developed'?

To help you swim like a fish, experts from the Natural History Museum were called in to study the ultimate underwater mover – the shark. They discovered that the feel and shape of a shark's skin varies across its body, enabling it to manage the flow of water and move with maximum efficiency. Not surprisingly, humans aren't built like that! But the new suit works on the same principle. It's made up of several different materials, designed to create a free-flowing, reduced-friction swimmer.

bag for wet kit, training diary. You may wish to use a swimming hat: they do have a performance advantage and can make it easier to manage your hair post-swimming.

If you haven't got flip-flops, bare feet will do!

## SKILLS

Let's work through some of the basic skills you will need to complete the swimming section of your triathlon. Experienced triathletes normally use front crawl as their preferred stroke because it is fast, efficient and compact, requiring little space in the water which, in an open water competition at the higher level, is especially important. There are, however, no rules to dictate which stroke you have to use in your event and you can use whichever is most comfortable for you. If you have more ambitious aspirations then learning the front crawl may be worth considering but is certainly not essential. If you cannot swim there are lots of swimming classes for adults and many swimming

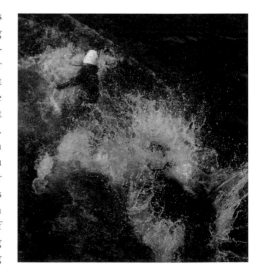

instructors will run one-to-one sessions if you feel this is the best option for you. Most local authority pools will offer this service as will many commercial gyms. You may need to allow yourself some extra time to work through this programme, adding the time you spend learning how to swim onto the total time for the programme.

In other training manuals you will find a great deal of detail on improving your swimming stroke. Our aim within this book is to help you complete a triathlon and therefore our goals and targets are a little different.

Space doesn't allow us to cover all the various techniques in detail but it may be worth contacting your local pool to seek help should you feel that your swimming technique is not sufficient to get you through your chosen event.

You will probably be swimming between 400 and 750 metres and our focus for the training programme will be to build up competently and comfortably to cover this distance as efficiently as possible. This is a principle that is applied to triathletes of all ability and will be a sound approach for our goal of completing the event.

## Front crawl: the basic technique

- A good catch point. This is where the propulsion through the water begins. The arm enters the water smoothly and travels a short distance forwards under the water before the hand will 'catch'. The hand starts to feel the resistance of the water and then

pulls against it, moving the hand and arm underneath the head and body. It is important not to start the pulling action too fast but to press with your fingers and have a firm wrist. This allows your hand to feel for the pressure of the water.

- High elbow position. Your hand stays still while the elbow moves over the hand as the shoulder rotates, allowing you to scull your hand laterally and vertically. The high elbow position ensures that a correct position is held throughout this action and is more a symptom of good technique rather than a cause and therefore this must be combined with all the other aspects discussed here.
- Swimmer to use sweeps. Use lots of sculling drills while the hand is moving through the water to encourage holding the 'pressure' throughout the propulsive effort and therefore generate a forward movement in the way that you would move forwards if on your back in the water using just the hands (no arm movement) to generate propulsion. This is often described as an S-pull, as the hand and arm track an elongated S through the water.
- Acceleration. Start each pull through the water with the hand and arm slowly, first feeling for the pressure and then accelerating through the propulsive pulling phase until the hand and arm exit the water.

The shape of the human body is not designed to move through water. It appears as though we swim on the surface of the water but actually we swim *through* the surface. The potential for negative resistant force (drag) is extremely high. Four types of drag will hold you back:

- Form drag – this is caused by the size and shape of the body as it is presented to the water.

- Wave drag – this is caused by the waves you make as you move through the water and the action of the waves against you.
- Frictional drag – friction between your body and swimwear and the surrounding water molecules.
- Eddy currents – the tendency of water to fill in behind you as you move forwards, therefore generating a drag to pull you backwards with the moving water.

To help eliminate as much drag as possible you need to present as little frontal mass to the water as possible, so effective streamlining is essential. The coach should train you to swim in two straight lines:
- A horizontal line from head to feet is desirable: the straighter this line, the less form drag and wave drag.
- A vertical plane when the swimmer is viewed from behind or above and from head to feet is also desirable.

Any side-to-side movement of the body will increase form drag, wave drag and eddy currents. Because of the relative slow speed of swimming, frictional drag is not as critical. Using a triathlon-specific wetsuit and a swim hat will probably be sufficient to help you reduce frictional drag. Some races use a personal timing chip, which is a small piece of plastic that links to the electronic timing system to give athletes a race time. This is often placed around the ankle on a strap. It needs to be carefully positioned to ensure that it is not uncomfortable and does not present too much drag.

The shape and orientation of the body in the water will determine how much resistance will be encountered; the more tapered and slender the shape the better. A tapered shape disrupts the water less, presents less frontal mass and allows the water molecules to fill in

theory. If an athlete swims three times as fast they will not just create three times as much resistance. They will actually create resistance depending on the square of their swim speed and so they create nine times as much. Technique and streamlining help to reduce drag as your speed increases and good pace will leave you with more energy to overcome drag towards the end of the swim section and throughout the rest of the triathlon.

almost immediately after the body passes through the water. Fish obviously have the ideal shape for moving through water; unfortunately, compared to fish the human body shape is poorly designed for this purpose. Furthermore, swimmers change position constantly as they swim, presenting a variety of shapes to the oncoming water flow. You should aim to reduce these variations to an absolute minimum and eliminate any unnecessary movement.

When you increase your speed in the water you create more turbulence and increase your drag. The faster you swim the more resistance you create. Speed in the water is governed by what is known as the Theoretical Square Law

# FOCUS ON OLYMPIC TRIATHLON

The summer Olympics in Sydney in 2000 was a turning point for the sport of triathlon. This was the first time that it was included in the Olympics. The race distance was:

* Swim: 1500 metres
* Bike: 40 kilometres
* Run: 10 kilometres

This is also the distance over which the International Triathlon Union (ITU) runs its world championships.

The race in Sydney was run over a good testing course and as one of the early events in the games it got fantastic viewing figures which contributed to the growth of triathlon across the world. It is now considered to be one of the fastest growing Olympic sports and the events in Athens in 2004 over a very challenging course showed the growth of the sport both in terms of the television viewing figures and, more importantly, the number of nations now taking part. At this level the sport is slightly different as drafting (riding very close to the rider in front) is allowed, where it is not in novice and age group races. This does give a very different type of event but one that is no less of a physical challenge or sporting spectacle, especially when tactics are considered as well as the physical aspects of the sport.

There is now a campaign to get triathlon included in the Paralympics programme to give the same kind of boost to athletes with impairments and give them a world stage.

# TECHNIQUE

## Overview

Front crawl is the fastest of the four competitive strokes and is the most energy efficient, hence it is the stroke most recommended for overall conditioning. It is an essential skill for triathletes, as speed and energy efficiency are important in multi-sport events. With this stroke, the net force is directed backwards and there is continuous propulsion. Being better streamlined than any other, the stroke is highly efficient, particularly for long-distance events such as the Ironman. The following description is not a definitive explanation of the stroke but is a guide to the basics which are required to swim the stroke at a competitive level.

## Body position

Your body should be as flat, horizontal and streamlined as possible, just below the surface of the water. Your head should be in line with your body, in a relatively natural position, i.e. not lifted or looking down. Your eyes should be looking diagonally forwards and down (at an angle of around 45°) and the water breaking at your forehead just above eyebrow level. It is essential that your head should remain still and central during the stroke cycle to prevent excess turbulence, except when breathing. Your shoulders and hips should be high in the water, with your feet just below the surface. Rotation around the long axis is required to allow effective propulsive movements of the arms and legs, and to help breathing action.

It is important to encourage full rotation of your body so that your hips and shoulders roll together and you avoid the problem of what is known as 'fixed' hips. Correct body rolling technique can make the front crawl action much more streamlined and efficient. This rolling motion not only makes the stroke look more effortless, but it actually makes it easier to perform. Your body must be kept horizontal in the water as much as possible when viewed from the side and a vertical/straight line when viewed from above or behind.

## Leg action

Leg action and head position are two fundamental components of an effective body position in the water. The main role of the leg action is to balance the propulsive movements of your arms and maintain a streamlined body position. Variations of the kick are possible. For example, two beat, four beat, six beat – the number refers to the number of times the legs are kicked for every stroke the arms perform. Triathletes who compete in sprint distance events tend to favour a higher beat leg kick, whilst Ironman competitors tend to adopt a two- or four-beat kick, as that uses less energy. Many triathletes believe that the kick is not an important component of the stroke for swimming. This is not true; the kick plays a major part in maintaining correct body position so the use of the legs is essential. It is true that when using a wetsuit the legs will naturally be more buoyant but a good efficient kick is still necessary. Ankle flexibility is also of great importance to the effectiveness of the kick both for propulsion and balance.

## Downbeat

The kick starts from the hips; the thigh is swept downwards as the foot passes the line of the hip during the previous upbeat. The knee and ankle joints should be relaxed with the foot held in a plantar-flexed position. The whip-like action towards the end of the downbeat results in the legs snapping straight. This whip-like action brings the largest area of the feet in contact with the water pressure in a backwards and downwards direction. Some in-toeing (a situation where the toes are pointing in towards the centre-line of the body) can occur during this phase.

## Upbeat

The leg should be extended and straight with the foot in a slightly dorsi-flexed position and rebound upwards as the previous downbeat is completed. The thigh starts the up kick and the knee flexes slightly. The foot is plantar-flexed before the start of the downbeat. A good coaching tip is to keep your leg fairly straight on the up beat to avoid excessive bending of the knees.

The kick should be maintained within the body depth (about 30–45cm). If this range is extended, then unnecessary resistance can occur.

## Limb path

It is important that the kick is not entirely on a vertical plane but moves with the hip rotation created by the body roll. The kick will move through a diagonal and vertical direction.

## Arm action

The main propulsive force of the front crawl is derived from the arms and is an alternating action with continuous movement. Your hand enters the water in front of your head and in line with your shoulders, about half way between the shoulder and fully extended arm length. Your hand should be angled at approximately 35° with a clean, thumb-first entry. Your hand is extended forwards, just below the water surface, to full extension but without overreaching.

## Down-sweep

Your hand sculls outwards and downwards to the catch point. Your hand resists the pressure of the water and your shoulder medially rotates to raise the elbow (high elbow). Your hand then continues to sweep outwards and downwards.

## In-sweep

Your elbow increases in flexion and the pitch of your hand turns inwards. Your hand sweeps inwards and acceleration of your hand increases.

## Up-sweep

Your hand pitch adjusts again to a backwards and outwards position. Your fingers point down until the final stages as the hand sweeps up, out and back. Acceleration continues. When your hand passes your hips, your wrist rotates and releases the water. Your hand is now in position for exit.

## Sweeping movement

When viewed from below, your hand should follow the S-shape pull pattern. The severity of the S will depend on individual characteristics such as strength.

## Recovery

This should be made with high elbows and no tension in your hands or arms. Your fingers should point down and your hand should start to reach for entry once your arm passes your head.

# Breathing

Breathing in swimming has to be taught and, for the non-swimmer, it can be quite challenging. Your head should rotate gradually as your arm is pulled back. Breathing should be at the end of the propulsive phase of the arm with your head as low as possible. You should breathe in the bow wave created by your head. Your head should turn at approximately 45° to the side, so you are looking at the poolside wall, and return smoothly and without delay following breathing. Your face should be back in the water before your arm passes your head during the recovery phase. Bilateral breathing should be encouraged even if the swimmer does not use it in a race; the ability to breathe to both sides is very important and will remove a potential handicap. In open water, if you are only capable of breathing to one side you may be disadvantaged if the wind or waves come from the direction in which you are breathing. The ability to breathe to the other side will be invaluable in this situation. Bilateral breathing encourages the return of the head to the central position and is good for stroke balance and control. The swimmer should breathe out gradually underwater with full exhalation at the end of the pulling phase of the arm.

## Timing

Different timing of the kick to the arms is possible. Two-beat, four beat, six-beat and two-beat crossover kicks are used. Essentially this means the number of kicks in relation to the number of arm strokes. Some swimmers will naturally kick more slowly than others. The six-beat kick is generally more propulsive but also uses more energy and many distance swimmers use reduced kicks and then increase the kick rate towards the end of the race. The important thing with kicking and timing is that it must balance the sweeping action of the arm and keep the body in alignment so that less resistance is created.

## Pool-based or open water swimming

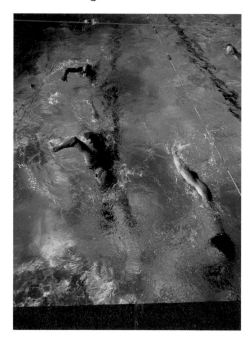

Your first event will almost certainly be a pool-based triathlon. If it is not, you will experience an additional challenge as open water swimming requires additional skills that we will touch on below.

You will be given a start time to be on the poolside; guidance may also be given about what other equipment you can take to the poolside but you will probably not be able to take very much kit. You will have to walk from the swim to the transition area in bare feet, though the surface will have been prepared for this. You may want to take a towel or T-shirt, if allowed, which will help you dry off a little before the next section of the event.

Once on the poolside you will be instructed to enter the water and then either counted down to start or given a 'ready, steady, go'. Your race time will be taken from this point. You will not be allowed to dive start. You may find that you are sharing the lane with another competitor. This is not something to worry about as you will probably have been training in a pool used by other people and will inevitably have swum next to other people in the course of your preparations but you should be aware of overtaking etiquette.

If you are sharing a lane you will be given explicit instructions about which direction to swim in, as lanes are normally organised to swim down the pool on one side of the lane and back up the pool on the other side. This is also common practice in public pools during laned swimming sessions, so you will have had an opportunity to get used to this. You are unlikely to have access to ladders at the pool either for entry or exit and therefore you will need to practise getting in and out from pool height.

You will probably swim a set number of lengths or, in some events, swim down one lane and then back up another until you have crossed the width of the pool from your point of entry to the point of exit. You are entirely responsible for ensuring that you cover the correct distance, though there is often a helper present to ensure that you are not going too far, or perhaps more seriously, not far enough.

For open water swimming, you will probably need to be a more confident and proficient swimmer because the distances will be towards the longer end of our range of sprint distance events.

Whether to swim in a wetsuit or not also needs to be really thought out. Although we didn't cover wetsuits in our equipment section, the choice and selection of this piece of kit is going to be crucial as a swimming-specific wetsuit makes your job a lot easier and a lot safer.

You will need to be able to navigate in the water and have practised this skill before the event. If you are swimming front crawl this will require a partial break of stroke to look up and around to see your navigational marker, which will either be a buoy or the swim exit. You may also want to consider practising the start as you will probably have to tread water for several minutes before being started by a gun or hooter. At that point you have to go from treading water to moving forwards, a task that is quite a challenge and needs practising. These are probably the two key points of open water swimming. Many triathlon clubs run open water training sessions which give you the opportunity to get used to the sensation of swimming in open water and also the chance to practise these two key techniques, both of which are important regardless of which stroke you use.

Many people take swimming for pleasure for granted. They probably learned to swim as children and only really swim on holidays. Working towards your first triathlon will mean you swim more often and with a very real purpose. Swimming probably has the lowest risk of injury of the three disciplines but this does not mean you won't ache from all that work in the pool. It can be a little monotonous but the hours in the water will pay off in the race.

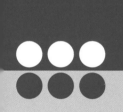

3

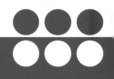

# cycling

## EQUIPMENT

### Clothing

There is one item of cycling clothing that will transform your cycling experience: cycling shorts. They come in a wide variety of designs but regardless of which design you opt for or how much you pay they will make your cycling more comfortable. They prevent chafing, reduce saddle soreness and keep you warm.

You can normally buy cycling shorts from the larger sports retailers but a trip to a good cycling shop will give you a wider range of products and, more importantly, you will benefit from the advice and expertise of the staff who know their products and know the sport. Cycling shorts come in two main designs: the normal short type that finishes with a high waist and bid shorts. Bid shorts cover more of the lower back and don't have elastic around the waist which some people find annoying when they are cycling. They are normally more expensive but as this will be your most important piece of cycling clothing don't be too tight with your budget. Shorts are assessed by the number of panels they have, and by the quality of the saddle insert (padding) and the quality of the material. The leggings you use for running can also be used for cycling in colder weather. You can buy specific cycling leggings which may be more suitable and comfortable, but your budget will dictate if you feel this investment is suitable for you. There are also many cycling tops from short-sleeved racing tops through to expensive all-weather jackets. A cycling jersey goes over the technical T-shirt we use when running, providing you with the characteristic handy rear pockets. Again, you can spend a great deal of money on this kind of clothing but your local cycling retailer will help you find suitable items. Of course a waterproof jacket is a good idea to help you on those damp days and the high visibility items you will also use for running will be useful when cycling, where it is arguably more important.

## Helmets

When considering safety equipment the cycle helmet is, of course, the most important piece of equipment. These are available from many retailers though again a good bike shop will help you select a quality item. Make sure it carries the CE mark – indicating the European safety standard – as this is a requirement for all races in the UK and you may be checked. Make sure that your helmet is a good fit and that the straps are adjusted to give a snug fit to stop it moving during cycling, especially if you have an accident. The other item that will offer protection in an accident is a pair of gloves. In winter they will help to keep you warm, while fingerless cycling gloves called track mitts are ideal for summer. Gloves can also add to your comfort by absorbing the minor bumps and vibration through the handlebars.

There are a number of other international cycling standards that are acceptable to race organisers. These include SNELL and ANSI. Your helmet should have one of these marks or a CE mark on it to ensure that it is suitable and safe for you to wear while racing.

## FITTING YOUR HELMET

Your helmet should fit your head well and be snug before you attempt to do up the chin strap. Most helmets come in a range of sizes so different head shapes and sizes can

usually be accommodated. A good bike shop is the best place to buy a helmet so you can try it on and get the advice you need, as well as making sure you look good it in!

The helmet should sit level on your head. This is achieved using the internal padding and the strapping at the back of the head, not the chin strap. The chin strap should simply secure the helmet in position rather than force it into position. The chin strap should be snug and have room for no more than two fingers between the strap and underneath the chin.

## The clipless pedal

Your choice of footwear will depend on your bike; there are many types of specialist cycling shoes available which give a fixed position on the pedal. These are relatively specialised and not cheap so unless you are making a long-term investment in your cycling then they are probably not for you.

Clipless pedal systems will improve your performance and efficiency but they require a degree of skill to set up. Again your cycle shop will be able to help you here, though coaches at a local cycling or triathlon club may also be able to help you to select and set up the clipless pedal system. Most bikes come with either flat pedals or pedals with the more traditional clips and strap. These can be used with normal training shoes; some manufacturers produce a sports shoe with a stiffer sole to help with the pedalling action. You should probably avoid using your running shoes for cycling as the softer compound in the sole may suffer on the hard pedals and some of your energy will be lost in the compression of the soles. You can, of course, race in them and not feel the effects too badly or you can change your shoes in the transition from the cycling to the run section.

# TRIATHLON – A SPORT FOR ALL

As a developing sport, triathlon has grown in a number of areas. One of the most exciting is the development of the sport for athletes who have physical impairments or disabilities. As with able-bodied athletes, these sportspeople want to compete against others from similar backgrounds and triathlon has been quick to embrace the opportunity of developing triathlons that can accommodate athletes with all kinds of physical disabilities. We now regularly see athletes who have visual impairments, prosthetic limbs or who use wheelchairs. Events are designed to accommodate them

and rules are modified to allow them to take part and encourage them to compete. As it is now an Olympic sport it is surely just a question of time before triathlon is included in the Paralympic games, proving that triathlon can really accommodate everyone. For athletes to compete against others with similar impairments, there is a classification system which is based on a physical profile, the definitions of which can be found on the British Triathlon website or from the International Triathlon Union. The British Triathlon profile system is applied for classification as follows:

TRI 1 – Wheelchair users with arm impairment: swim, tricycle or hand cycle and wheelchair. Help allowed for transition. (Profiles 1, 2, 3, 4, 5, 6, 7)

TRI 2 – Severe impairment of two or more limbs: swim, tricycle, run. Help allowed for transition. (Profiles 12, 13, 14, 17a, 31, 32, 27)

TRI 3 – Wheelchair users with no or minimal arm impairment: swim, hand cycle, wheelchair. Help allowed for transition. (Profiles 8, 9, 10, 11, 17b, 18a)

TRI 4 – Severe impairment of one lower limb, or moderate impairment of two lower limbs, or minimal impairment of four limbs: swim, cycle, run. (Profiles 18b,19a, 20a, 26, 28, 25)

TRI 5 – Impairment in one or both upper limbs: swim, cycle, run. (Profiles 16, 21, 22)

TRI 6 – Slight impairment of one or two limbs: swim, cycle, run. (Profiles 15, 19b, 20b, 23, 24, 29)

TRI 7 – Totally blind and partially sighted as defined by BBS (British Blind Sport): swim, tandem, run (all with guide). (Profiles 36, 37a, 37b)

TRI 8 – Learning impairment as defined by UK SAPLD (UK Sports Association for People with Learning Disability): swim, cycle, run. (Profile 39)

TRI 9 – Hearing impairment as defined by Deaflympics and British Deaf Sports: swim, cycle, run in age group categories. (Profile 38)

## Setting your cycle up correctly

Bikes come in many different designs and types and almost any bike can be used for your triathlon. It is very common to see shopping bikes, mountain bikes and hybrid bikes in novice events and these can be great to train on as you will be able to train on different surfaces, which will make your training more interesting. This piece of triathlon equipment can be the biggest investment but it is not necessary if you already have a bike, which you can either use as it is or with a few minor adjustments to make it a faster, more efficient machine. Whilst we don't have room in this book to help you become an expert on bikes and bike design, it is worthwhile going through some basics of the bike to help you train.

Regardless of what type of bike you are riding, it must be safe and roadworthy. This means that you should be able to go through the following checklist before you start riding:

- Handlebars – pointing in the correct direction and tight in position.
- Steering – turns without hindrance and without slack.
- Saddle – pointing in the correct direction and firmly fixed.
- Brakes – easily operated by pulling the levers, which should operate without hindrance and without the lever touching the bars. The brakes should lock with ease.
- Chain – this should be well lubricated, not rusty.
- Chainset – no lateral play (movement from side to side).
- Pedals – they should spin easily and with no lateral play.
- Gears – these should operate correctly without disengaging the chain from either the chainset or the rear sprockets.
- Wheels – should spin freely and without noise with all spokes tightened firmly and the rim not wobbling noticeably. There should not be any play in the hub.

- Tyres – There should be plenty of rubber on the tyre and the sidewalls should be in good repair without any canvas showing. The tyres should also be at the right pressure; this can be checked using a gauge. The recommended pressure will be printed on the side of the tyre but a general check is to squeeze the tyre from the side where a small amount of movement should be felt.
- The frame – this is the heart of the bike and it should be sound and without visible cracks or strains.

The easiest way to check your bike for road worthiness is to give it a clean using a spray lubricant such as GT85 on the moving parts. It is also a good idea to have your bike serviced by a good bike shop before training to make sure it is safe, especially if it has been standing for some time.

If you are considering buying a bike for your event then there is a great deal of choice from mountain bikes and hybrids through to the more specialist racing bikes. Your local retailer will understand your needs and, knowing your budget, can advise you on your best options. If you are planning to use your bike for commuting and social riding then a hybrid bike or mountain bike is probably best. If your

aims are purely sporting then a racing-style bike may be better. Regardless of the type of bike you choose it must be a good fit. If you are buying from a shop you will get suitable advice there, but if you already have your own bike then you need to follow the guidelines below.

## FOOT POSITION

Incorrect foot positioning can very quickly lead to injury. The foot is a fundamental area of power transfer and therefore achieving the correct position is vital. The centre of the ball of the foot should be directly over the centre of the pedal spindle and the foot should normally be parallel with the cranks (see page 152). This is the optimum position for high power output and a high cadence, though there may be circumstances when this position varies. For example, some cyclists may find a 'heels in' or 'heels out' position to be more natural and comfortable. As long as this is established as being a natural tendency then this is acceptable. To assess the natural foot position, sit on a table with your legs dangling. From this, you will see your natural foot position.

## SADDLE HEIGHT POSITION AND TILT

This is probably the most important measurement when fitting your bike. This figure has, in the past, been tied very closely to frame size. With the increasing popularity of compact design frames and the possibility that you will have a bike other than a standard road bike, this measurement is no longer as useful. To arrive at an optimum saddle height we need first to measure the inside leg (or inseam). Once you have this measurement, the frame size and saddle height can be calculated by the following formula:

For saddle height, multiply the rider's inseam by 0.885.

For example: inseam of 83cm x 0.885 = 73.5, therefore saddle height should be 73.5cm to the centre of the bottom bracket.

When this figure is applied to the bike, the rider's leg should not be locked out. It should have a slight bend at the knee when the pedal is in line with the seat tube.

There are numerous other formulae that can be applied to achieve the same result, for example multiplying the rider's inseam by 1.09 to calculate the saddle height. This figure will also include the crank arm.

This calculation can be varied slightly to

allow for anatomical differences, particularly between male and female riders. The degree of variance should not exceed 0.03. Therefore the lowest calculation you should complete is 'inseam x 1.06', and the highest calculation that should be completed is 'inseam x 1.12'.

Once you have arrived at your optimum measurement this needs to be applied to the bike. The measurement you have relates to distance between the top of the saddle and the centre of the pedal axle. Slight alteration may be needed for the pedal and shoe combination and the type. Additional factors that may affect this measurement are clothing – thickness and type; leg length discrepancies; flexibility; bicycle type and design, including suspension where fitted, and pedalling style.

The simplest method to determine saddle height is for the rider to sit on their bike with their heels on the pedals. Set the pedal to its lowest position (in line with the seat tube) and the leg should be straight, without overstretching. It is important to note that there should be no rocking of the hips from side to side. This position may, however, be too low for many cyclists, so you may have to raise the saddle by 1–2cm to achieve the most comfortable position.

Once the correct saddle height has been achieved, the position and tilt of the saddle then need to be considered. Saddle position is measured relative to the bottom bracket (crank axle) and the rails of the saddle allow fore and aft movement. The angle of the seat tube of the bike frame will play an important role in this adjustment; you may

find seat tube angles vary from 70° through to 75° to the horizontal. A reliable measurement is to take a plumb line and see if the cyclist's knee sits over the pedal axle when the cranks are horizontal.

Saddles should be set parallel to the ground or with a very slight upward tilt at the nose. This will vary slightly depending on the shape of the saddle used. If the nose of the saddle tilts down too much, weight will be pushed onto the arms causing undue fatigue and discomfort. Many women tilt the saddle down in an attempt to reduce the pressure on the groin. In this instance, look for a more suitable saddle. A saddle that tilts up usually indicates that it is too low and conversely a saddle tilting down may indicate that it is a little too high. Check the

saddle height as discussed and re-adjust as necessary.

You should be looking for a position which maintains the position of your hips and legs in relation to the pedals and bottom bracket, whilst allowing you to lower the position of your head and shoulders and bring your arms closer together. This may take a little trial and error but, providing you are moving at speeds in excess of around 16mph, the effects will be advantageous. Riding in this position obviously compromises the amount of control you can exert over the bike and therefore it is only on straight roads where you have a good degree of visibility and are aware of potential risks that riding like this should be undertaken. Practising first on a static training device (turbo trainer) or on quiet roads will help you to become accustomed to the position.

## STEM HEIGHT, EXTENSION, HANDLEBAR WIDTH AND POSITION

Stem height is the height of the stem holding the handlebars in place; extension refers to its length, or the distance forward that the stem extends. This measurement again has its limitations, as the angle of the foot will vary throughout the pedal revolution depending on individual technique. Many successful cyclists and triathletes have used knee positions that sit forwards of this point. For this reason allow a variance of 2cm from the plumb line.

Reach is the distance between the centre of the saddle and the centre of the handlebars. This is governed by both the length of the stem and the adjustment of the saddle rails forward and aft. Influencing factors on this measurement are the length of the cyclist's arms and back, the degree of flexibility and size of their hands, and the position they are trying to achieve. Once pedal and saddle height position and tilt have been established, the only factors that have influence over the reach are frame size (non-adjustable), stem length and handlebar selection.

For drop bars, although cyclists may spend a greater degree of time on the tops of the bars or on the brake hoods, they should be able to reach the drops quite comfortably.

The bottom section of the bars should be parallel with the floor or tilted upwards slightly. When on the drops, the cyclist should have a slight bend at the elbow to allow some suspension of the body; if the arms are locked straight, road shock is transferred directly through the handlebars, arms and body. The elbow should just clear the knee (a gap of 1–4cm) when the crank is at its most forward position. This should leave the back nearly horizontal without causing the cyclist to move forwards on the saddle.

Women may need less reach because of their relatively shorter torso and arms. Because of this they will also have less difference between saddle and handlebar height. However, as women generally have a greater degree of flexibility they may be able to tolerate a greater difference.

While this greater degree of difference will result in a much flatter back and may prove aerodynamic, it will probably lead to a loss of power and leverage. The use of tri-bars and/or low profile bars is also commonplace in triathlon. These bars are designed to lower the frontal area that you present to the wind. By doing this you can become more aerodynamic and subsequently faster. Many triathletes adjust the position to such an extent that it has a detrimental effect on the critical measurements surrounding the position of the body in relation to the pedals and therefore they sacrifice efficiency and the transfer of power is reduced. To prevent this you must be very careful when setting up any such bars.

## The bicycle explained

### FRAME MATERIALS

Traditionally bicycle frames were constructed using steel tubing. The tubes were joined using lugs and were brazed together. Frame materials have changed considerably in the last twenty-five years and frames are now made from aluminium, titanium and carbon fibre.

Each material has its benefits in terms of ride comfort and handling but for many the major benefit in the change in frame materials has been the ability to reduce the weight of the bicycle. Carbon fibre can produce a very light, very stable frame that can be built into a very light-weight bicycle. When first introduced carbon was very expensive but, as with most products, prices have gone down over time to now give a range of very light, affordable and reliable carbon fibre framesets. You certainly do not need a bike made this way to take part but many enthusiasts aspire to ride a carbon fibre bike.

### GEARS

As frames have improved so too have the number of gears available on racing and all types of bicycle. Initially this came from the increase in the number of sprockets on the rear hub of the bike. This was traditionally set at five but increased steadily over twenty-five years to eight, nine and now more commonly ten sprockets on the rear. This gives a good selection of gears without large jumps in gear ratios. This increase in sprockets and the development and adaptation of mountain bike technology has given us chain-sets with three chain-rings and a selection of gears that is very wide indeed and gives a huge amount of flexibility.

Gear selection methods have also altered. The first development was the introduction of indexing. Indexed gears had a ratchet mechanism in their levers which equated one click forward to one gear change. This method was a huge improvement on the feel method of changing gear which riders previously had to endure. The levers at this point were still located on the down tube of the bicycle frame and required the rider to take their hands off the bars to make the gear change. This was cumbersome and slow. Shimano was the first manufacturer to introduce an integrated gear and brake lever for the bicycle which operated the brake in the traditional method but with a sideways movement to make the gear change. Campagnolo followed very shortly with a similar system. You are now unlikely to see a racing bike without one of these systems.

Mountain and hybrid bikes all now have gear changing systems that do not require the rider to change hand position to change gear. There are two main systems: one is twistgrip, where part of the handlebar moves to change the gear with the right hand lever operating the rear changer and left hand lever operating the front. The second set of levers you may find on this type of bike is the quickshot system which has two levers on either side, one for changing up and one for changing down.

## BRAKES

You will come across three main types of brake callipers (the bit that squeezes the wheel).

Cantilever brakes have a two-part system on each wheel where a central straddle cable pulls them together to squeeze the rim. These brakes are found on cyclo-cross bikes and on some older mountain bikes. The other type of brakes more commonly found on mountain and hybrid bikes is the V-brake. These have two parts which are like long arms pointing up and when the lever is operated the cable pulls the two parts together putting pressure on the rim.

On road bikes you are more likely to find a brake calliper. This is fixed via a central drilling in the frame to hold the calliper in place. These are operated by a cable pulling the arms together via a central pivot or, as is more commonly the case now, a dual pivot which gives a greater, more efficient stopping power.

You may also see disc brakes. Again a development from the mountain bike world, these brakes are very effective and are either operated hydraulically, in the more expensive models, or by cable. Their operation is similar to that in a car and these brakes are very efficient though slightly heavier than the other systems.

## WHEELS

There are a huge number of different wheels available to the racing cyclist. Many entry level racing bikes are supplied with good quality wheels though the design and production of these wheels has changed a great deal recently. Many spokes are now flattened to be more aerodynamic and the method of lacing the spokes has also changed in many instances. Rim technology has also moved on with carbon fibre being used in preference to aluminium to produce lighter, more aerodynamic wheels, often with deeper rims. These wheels are great for time trialling and can be used in road racing but are more susceptible to side winds

and can be difficult to handle in a group situation when the weather is breezy. Wheel selection is again a very personal choice, with aesthetics and budget being the most important factors. You will come across a wide variety of wheel designs at most races and a quick chat with different users will give you an idea of the advantages and disadvantages of differing designs.

## The female-specific bike

There are differences in the way women and men are proportioned. On average, women have longer legs and shorter torsos, relative to their overall height. Much of this 'extra' length comes from the thigh bone which

tends to make up a higher percentage of leg length in women than in men. This is especially true in taller women who make up a significant percentage of the elite triathlete and cycling population. Women also tend to be, on average, shorter than men. More importantly, though, women generally have narrower shoulders and smaller feet and hands. What does this mean for bike design and set-up? Traditionally bikes were sized up simply according to inside leg length or 'stand-over height' (and in many shops they sadly still are). However, for most women this will lead to too big a frame given her proportionally longer legs relative to height and, in particular, torso length. What then happens is the unsuspecting woman is sold a short stem and an in-line seat pin to shorten the distance from saddle to handlebars. This is a highly unsatisfactory compromise. The handling of the bike will be deleteriously affected and the position of the knees relative to the feet (too far forwards) will cause poor power transfer and, probably, sore knees. All in all, an uncomfortable and unresponsive ride.

Current recommendations for sizing bicycles are more focused on top-tube length so many women are simply sold a smaller frame size in order to get the correct top tube length. But this in itself is only half the solution. Stem length and saddle position still need to be optimised. Also, there may not always be a smaller size frame available!

There is an increasing number of cycle manufacturers looking to cash in on the expansion in the marketplace by offering female-specific road bikes and other equipment. 'Women-specific geometry' is promoted as, in the main, a shorter top tube and smaller frame sizes. Whilst the latter is undoubtedly very helpful, the former may not necessarily be the answer: it depends on how this is achieved.

The simplest, and therefore cheapest, way to achieve a shorter bike top tube is to bring the seat tube forward, to bring the saddle closer to the handlebars. In practice this usually means making the seat tube more upright – steeper.

For maximal transmission of power from the contraction of the powerful thigh muscles to the pedals, the foot and knee must be properly aligned over the pedal spindle. Sitting too far forwards or back will result in inefficient power transmission and also risk knee pain.

As mentioned earlier, women tend to have relatively longer legs and in particular the thigh bone. Thus to achieve an optimal knee/foot/pedal position the rider will need to sit well behind the bottom bracket area. In these designs, where the top tube is created by steepening the seat tube, the opposite happens. So, our rider moves the saddle as far back as it will go. The reach is now again too long so she must buy a shorter handlebar stem and we are back to square one.

The best way to achieve a truly female-specific frame can only be achieved by redesigning the whole geometry to achieve a shorter top tube and a shallower seat tube angle. The leaders in this field have to be American Bicycle Group: designers and manufacturers of Quintano Roo, Merlin, and Litespeed. They have not only invested in a full geometrical redesign for their frames but also for a range of forks which give excellent race bike handling qualities even on smaller bikes.

## COMPONENTS AND ACCESSORIES

Finally we come to the array of female-specific components and accessories: which of these do we really need? Yes, narrower width bars will help optimise the riding position, make it more aerodynamic (smaller frontal area) and also take some of the strain off the shoulders but these bars also need to be shorter front to back. Shimano Ultegra shifter levers are available with an inset wedge to fit smaller hands and the new Dura Ace ones are shaped so that the risk of putting on the brakes whilst shifting gear is reduced.

However, in general, Campagnolo levers offer a better grip for smaller hands and are easier to operate from the brake hoods. Most women seem to prefer riding on the brake hoods to the drop-bar bends. This has often been assumed to be due to shorter reach (cf. the raised handlebar issue) but is undoubtedly due to smaller hands feeling more secure whilst braking from this position compared with fingertip-only contact from the drops. Crank and stem length need to be proportional to the bike and the rider not used as a way of adapting the bike to fit. A smaller woman with small feet will benefit from shorter cranks

– not for ease of spinning (the lighter muscles will aid that anyway) but simply to make the bike fit her!

## THE SADDLE

This is a sensitive area and an important subject. There can be the assumption that the bigger, more padded the saddle the more comfortable it will be. This is not always the case and for men a slim saddle, set up correctly, will often provide the best option. There are many saddles on the market and they will all take a little getting used to but talk to your bike dealer if you find trouble locating a comfortable saddle.

For women the selection can be more difficult. Women's wider hips do require a degree of support and you will find female-specific saddles of all shapes and sizes. Again trial and error may be required.

## Aerodynamic equipment and set-up

Over the past two decades there have been many improvements in aerodynamics for cycling. This has included wheels, frames, handlebars and rider clothing. The basic design of the bicycle is relatively aerodynamic anyway, as it has a low profile, and it is in the area of clothing that the rider can make the most advances. Close-fitting clothing is the key, and the use of a specifically aerody-namic helmet can make a difference if you are riding at speeds faster than 30 kilometres per hour. There are many aerodynamic helmets on the market and they generally have a profile which is clearly designed to

make the passage through the air as easy as possible. This is often obvious by a point at the rear of the helmet extending down the back, though this is often at the expense of air vents which compromise ventilation.

The great thing about cycling is that there are a huge number of ways you can invest in equipment. There is often a debate about the merits of aerodynamics versus weight reduction with some riders taking all possible action to reduce the weight of their bike in the belief that a very light bike will be faster.

This can be the case over a particularly hilly course but is probably truer for a rider who is already quite light. A rider who spends hundreds of pounds on light-weight equipment but could easily stand to lose a kilo or so in weight may be better investing his money elsewhere. However, it is often the case that a shiny bike with some nice bits of carbon fibre or titanium makes the rider feel better and enjoy riding it more and this alone can make them go faster.

Aerodynamics for bicycles is often seen as a very expensive path to follow. Bikes are not allowed to have any kind of fairing (any kind of device that is not structural but is designed to shield the rider from the wind) on them and the largest object blocking the path of the air is the rider. Despite this, there are many adaptations you can legally make to your bicycle to make it faster through the wind. The benefit of these adaptations is normally only felt at speeds over 18 miles per hour and most novices won't be averaging this speed. By taking some basic actions you can reduce your drag to allow you to go faster. Sensible positioning of your drinks bottle and other accessories can really help; it is well worth doing this kind of thing before you start looking at more expensive measures. Making sure brake and gear cables are concealed is another simple way which is relatively cheap. The next step is to use handlebars with a more aerodynamic profile. These come in aluminium and the more expensive carbon fibre.

The type of bars you fit can also have a major impact by altering your position. This is achieved by the use of tri-bars. The handlebar extensions can be part of an aerodynamic handlebar system or can be added to normal handlebars of any bicycle. Many triathletes use them but few manage to achieve a position that is efficient and aerodynamically advantageous. The efficiency of the bike is still the most important thing and any adaptations to position must be done carefully to ensure that the position we discussed earlier is still achievable when you use the tri-bars. If you can't use the bars whilst maintaining the current saddle position then don't adjust the saddle to fit the bars, adjust the bars to fit the saddle position.

There is a wide range of aerodynamic frames available which are designed to accommodate the triathlon and time trial position. This is one of the more extreme adaptations to improve the aerodynamics and the price is probably going to be quite high. It may also make your bike difficult to ride outside the racing environment.

Wheels with deeper rims and/or a reduced number of spokes make them faster through the air. There are also wheels with flat or bladed spokes, while the most extreme kind of aerodynamic wheel is a solid disc. These are generally made from carbon fibre and are only allowed on the front of any bike. They are never cheap but in the right conditions they can be very, very fast. Deep-rimmed wheels are also fast and have the advantage of being less susceptible to side winds. Again, construction is normally carbon fibre.

It is possible to spend an astronomical amount of money improving bikes and for those that want to indulge themselves the list can be almost endless. It is always worth remembering that the single component that makes a bike faster is the rider.

## SKILLS

In this section we will build on the basic skills of balance and steering to help you train and race safely and effectively.

### Starting

The basic technique to start riding safely is as follows. With the bicycle next to the kerb and pointing in the direction of travel, place both your hands on the top of the handlebars. Look over your right shoulder to check for traffic, swing your right leg over the saddle and place your foot on the pedal, which should be at the two o'clock position. Move your bottom onto the saddle and then prepare to push down on the pedal and move off, looking over your right shoulder just before doing so to check the road is clear of passing traffic. Once moving, place your left foot onto the pedal and continue pedalling. This process is easiest when using a kerb for balance but you should also be able to do this without. Using clipless pedals will make this action a little more complicated but you need to become competent at getting the pedals clipped in as quickly as possible so you can pedal forwards without losing momentum. Make sure that the gear you move off in is suitable, neither too hard (high) nor too easy (low); the correct gear will enable you to push off with a little effort and give you enough momentum from the initial revolution so you have time to get your other foot clipped in.

The techniques for racing in your triathlon are not widely different. When in your event you will need to push your bike forwards to the mounting line – the line before which you cannot ride your bike. It is a basic safety rule. You will see experienced triathletes jump onto a moving bike or scoot along before getting on the bike. This is an advanced skill that you can build up to, but it is not necessarily required as it is purely time saving. As our goal may simply be completion of the event, this more advanced skill may not be a major priority for you as you learn a new set of skills.

## Braking

Having started off we need to feel confident that we can slow down and stop. The brakes are operated by the levers on the

bars; it is worth checking which lever operates which brake, as the balance between front and back brake is critical to operation at speed. Most UK bikes have the front brake operated by the lever on the right hand side of the bars, though this may not be the case with the bike you are riding so you need to be very aware of the levers and which brake calliper they operate. When braking to slow down on dry roads the emphasis should be slightly on the rear brake. You want to avoid the rear wheel locking up and a skid occurring. The front brake also needs to be used to balance the braking power. When you are trying to come to a stop then the front brake needs to be used more and a theoretical 60 per cent preference for the front brake will deliver the power required to come to a halt safely.

Wet surfaces or roads with unstable surfaces require a greater degree of caution and braking should be a lot more progressive to avoid skidding and ensure control is maintained at all times. Careful practice is required to build up confidence in knowing when and where to brake to ensure you are as efficient as possible. The last thing you want is to lose speed and momentum which you have spent a long time gaining or to fall off.

## Cornering

The process of cornering is not necessarily difficult but we want to corner at speed. To achieve this we need to combine the braking skills detailed above with some additional techniques. There are a number of considerations when looking at any given cornering situation.

Your key considerations are:
- Surface
- Entry speed
- Exit speed
- Fastest line
- Tyre condition

Your overall objective for any corner in a race is to get through the corner as quickly as possible and to lose as little speed as possible. There is a route through the corner, which is often referred to as the line. When you are riding alone on roads that are free of traffic you can use the perfect line. The perfect line is the one that is the straightest around any given corner or bend. This involves the process of straightening out the bend.

As you approach the corner move towards the opposite side of the road (or lane), having first checked that it is safe to do so. (Of course, you need to stay on your own side of the road so as to avoid breaking traffic laws.) You can then see the line through the corner; look towards it and start the turning process. By making sure the inside pedal is up, most of the cornering will be achieved through leaning. Once the centre of the corner or apex is reached, you will start to head towards the exit point where you will be almost fully upright and ready to accelerate.

Your body position is very important when cornering because the distribution of your weight will affect the handling of the bike through the bend. It is best to hold the handlebars at the lowest point and you must remain seated throughout the turn. Once in the corner the pedal nearest to the inside of the corner must be at the top of its revolution. Your knees should remain pointing forwards and your elbows should also remain in though your shoulder can be dropped

slightly to put weight in towards the centre of the corner. Lift your weight very slightly off the saddle and onto the outside pedal which will also aid with the positioning of your body.

You need to find somewhere to practise your cornering or follow a small training route that requires you to corner a lot. Cornering must become second nature and you should develop the ability to judge the appropriate speed for a corner without pushing so hard you meet the tarmac. Only practise of the basic skills above will develop the skill required.

## Changing gear

This section will not be able to tell you which gear you need to be in and when – that is something only you can tell when you're on the road – but this section will briefly outline the basic skills of changing gear. The purpose of changing gears is to allow you to use your body as efficiently as possible. Efficiency is achieved by pedalling at the correct speed – cadence – and is measured in the number of revolutions per minute of your feet on the pedals. It is generally accepted that the optimum cadence for performance is between 80 and 100 revolutions per minute. This is quite a wide range but it does provide enough flexibility to accommodate different styles of rider. The current fashion is for a brisker cadence and to do this you will need to push what is described as a lower gear.

Gears are generally called 'high' or 'low'; this refers to the distance that you travel for any given revolution – a low gear travels a shorter distance than a high gear which travels a longer distance. The easiest way of telling the difference between gears is that a gear that is easy to push around is very low and a gear that is hard to push is high. Most bikes now have between fourteen and twenty gears and will have a gear selector or mechanism on the rear cogs and a mechanism on the front chain-ring or chainset (where the pedals are attached). The rear cogs are usually called sprockets and the gear, which is defined as a ratio, is a combination of the size of the rear sprockets in number of teeth and the size of the chain-rings in the number of teeth. The greater the difference between the number of teeth on the sprockets and chain-ring the higher the gear will be and the further you will travel with each pedal revolution. There are usually two chain-rings at the front controlled by the gear selector on the left hand side of your bike (see equipment section) and you will have between seven and ten sprockets on the rear of the bike controlled by the gear selector on the right hand side of the bike. Minor changes in gear can be achieved by using the rear selector controlled by the right hand lever and major changes can be achieved by shifting chain-rings using the left hand selector.

Most races, other than very hilly ones, will require the large chain-ring to be used almost exclusively with adjustments to accommodate terrain or pace made using the rear sprockets and rear mechanism controlled by the right hand lever.

Gears should be used to make the bike and rider as efficient as possible and to do this you should be using your gears to maintain a cadence of 80–100 revolutions per minute. You can buy a cycle computer to fix to your bike which will show you the cadence you are achieving. Alternatively, a count over a set period (15 or 30 seconds is best) will give you a pretty good idea. You will then get a feel for your natural cadence and therefore understand what needs to be done to increase this to be more efficient. This may feel unnatural due to the change of action for the legs but will pay dividends in the long run.

When changing gear a well-adjusted bike will, once directed by the lever, change quite efficiently. A slight easing of the pressure applied to the pedals will help the chain while it is moving through. This is more important when moving to a lower gear (or changing down) than it is when moving to a higher gear (or changing up). Anticipation is often a better tactic and by assessing what gear is required before it is needed you will be able to set the bike up and adjust your cadence as required.

Many entry level road bikes will have the range of gears required to accommodate racing. If you are riding in especially hilly events or very fast flat events you may want to consider looking at the gears you have. Similarly, if you are the kind of rider who discovers they have a talent for sprinting at the end of a road race, the gears available to you may also need to be looked at. A higher top gear will allow you to sprint or pedal at a lower cadence for a given speed but it may require too much effort to push to be economical for somebody who naturally pedals at a higher cadence.

The jump between gears is also a consideration and in flat time trials and many road races subtle adjustments are all that are required to maintain economy of effort. To help with this, a rear set of sprockets (often referred to as a block and which has very small differences in size between adjacent sprockets) would be more suitable. Changing these sprockets is not a difficult job, but for the novice the help of their cycle shop would be the best option as they will be able to help with compatibility of parts to ensure your bike still runs smoothly.

# Climbing

Regardless of where you live you will, at some point, come across a climb. This may only be a slight rise over a major road or motorway, or it could be a ten kilometre drag to the top of an alpine pass. There will obviously be a significant difference in your approach to these two different ascents but you do need to consider your physical and mental approach to climbs along with understanding your physical ability and limitations.

Your gear selection is vital for climbing, and ensuring you have the right gears for the race is important. Understanding your abilities when climbing is also a very important part of the way you approach a climb. In the UK you will find some climbs that take very little time to achieve but are relatively steep. This type of climbing uses a different energy system in the body to that used for longer climbs. This is more like an uphill sprint and therefore somebody who is not a light, natural climber may find that they ascend this type of climb more slowly than the lighter rider. The power to weight ratio will become more important on longer climbs and in this instance a degree of pacing is required to ensure that you get to the top. Your weight is an obvious factor affecting your ability to climb and by reducing this and increasing your power output (how hard you can pedal) you will climb faster. It may be that your natural physique does not lend itself to climbing quickly; a rider over six feet tall will struggle to reduce their weight to that of a rider just over five feet.

Go out and ride hills. By training hard and eating well your weight will reduce and your power will increase. Training with friends will help with your training as they will ride at different paces and this will help you to push yourself.

## Road safety

When you are racing, you will be directed around the course by marshals. These are normally volunteers who have an interest in the sport and help race organisers on the day to ensure that the events are safe. Always treat the marshals well and even if you are having a tough time, smile and say thanks if you have the breath to do so. Regardless of the marshals, you are responsible for finding your way around the course and you are certainly responsible for ensuring that you ride in accordance with the Highway Code. Many people worked through the cycling proficiency test when at school and a quick brushing up of the basic rules for cyclists will be very useful and will make sure that you don't get into difficulties.

Cycling on open roads can be a little daunting and there is no getting away from the fact that traffic volumes have increased greatly. A sensible approach to other road users will help to keep you safe, as will equipment such as gloves and high visibility jackets.

The end of the cycle section of the race is a reversal of the start. As you approach the dismounting line you must be off your bike before you cross the line. You must then move back to the space in the transition area allocated for your bike and put your bike on the rack before taking off your helmet. You can then move on to the run section.

When training for this element of triathlon you will be refining some skills from your

youth and developing some new ones. You will be using your bike as more than just leisure transport and will be moving into the world of the sporting cyclist. Developing a relationship with your bike shop will really help you with equipment selection, repairs and upgrades. Cycling can help you with transport and leisure time and the benefits of training for your triathlon can be felt across your lifestyle.

4

# running

## EQUIPMENT

### Footwear

Running requires one piece of equipment on which you should not skimp or try to save money. The footwear that you use for running will help prevent aches and pains or long-term injuries. There are many sports shops that will sell you a pair of training shoes; however, you need a sports shop that understands running and has knowledgeable and experienced staff. This is probably not one of the large chain sports clothing shops but is likely to be a local running or triathlon specialist shop. They will have a good degree of knowledge of the demands placed on a sports shoe during an endurance run. Regardless of the distance of your event you need an endurance running shoe not a cross-training shoe. You will also receive advice on the specific style of shoe you need based on where you run and your weight. You may also be fortunate enough to have your foot strike tested. This is an analysis of the way your foot strikes the floor when you run. It enables the shop staff to see if there are any areas where you need specific support by the way your foot lands when you run. This can simply be a case of improving the comfort of the shoe, which will prevent aches and pains caused by using muscles that are not normally used. If your foot strike is sufficiently unbalanced it can lead to injury; if you find you are experiencing pain in your knees or hips then this could be the cause. You will find that you can buy shoes that look like running shoes from your average sports shop but they won't necessarily be designed specifically for running and probably won't have the support that you require.

Running presents the greatest potential for injury of all three disciplines and it is vital that you choose the correct footwear. Your running shop will be able to advise you how often your shoes should be changed – many runners use more than one pair of shoes during an event so they are never running in damp footwear and to give the shoes a chance to recover from the multiple compressions they will deal with in even a short run. Buying in this way, if you can afford it, has many benefits, including that you will always have comfortable shoes and not have to get used to a different design when you replace your worn-out footwear.

Moving up from the shoes, socks are the next consideration. In triathlon most experienced competitors will certainly race, if not train, without socks. To many novices this seems entirely alien and also quite uncomfortable. Not wearing socks during a race will make your transition from swim to run much faster but may cause blisters during the run and bike sections.

There are plenty of very experienced and successful athletes who started their triathlon career putting socks on after the swim. Apart from the obvious problem of getting a sock onto a slightly damp foot while standing in a transition area, you should not be afraid of putting on socks at this point if you feel it is best for you. If you decide you are going to race without socks then you will need to do at least some training without them. Mention this to your footwear retailer as there are some specialist triathlon shoes which take sockless running into account in their design, avoiding any of the rougher seams that sometimes exist on less considerate footwear. The use of talcum powder will also make sockless running easier both in terms of getting the shoe on and preventing rubbing during the run. If you are using socks, you need a sports sock which has no seams; if you have particularly sensitive feet then running socks, will provide a greater degree of protection against blisters and will dry faster. They are more expensive than conventional socks but depending on your needs they may be worth the investment. Running with blisters is not a lot of fun and can be painful and more importantly will have a negative impact on your ability to train.

A common problem for those involved in running is pain or discomfort in the foot, ankle or knee, which is caused by pronation. Pronation is the excessive turning in of the foot as it approaches and strikes the ground. There is some natural turn in for the foot on most occasions, but excessive pronation can cause a number of issues including the stretching of soft tissues and the flattening of arches. Many good running shops have equipment that can identify this issue and they are often able to provide running shoes that are specifically adapted to accommodate a runner who pronates.

## Other clothing

Other clothing for running is just a case of being sensible and comfortable. There are also safety considerations so visibility must also be taken into account. As in swimming, close-fitting running wear is probably going to be both the most comfortable and the most effective. Large billowing tops and Bermuda shorts will create wind resistance so you should avoid this kind of outerwear. Most sports shops will provide clothing suitable for running and depending on your fashion requirements you should be able to find something comfortable. The time of year will play a huge part in your selection with summer runners opting for shorts. These are either the traditional looser-fitting but very short running shorts or the increasingly popular Lycra close-fitting shorts of varying length from short ones, generally more popular with women, through to almost knee-length garments. In the winter these

shorts can be replaced or augmented by some long tracksuit bottoms. Experienced runners often wear close-fitting trousers or leggings often referred to as Ron Hills. This is the brand name of designed leg wear and they are very good, but there are now many other brands producing similar close-fitting run leggings. These are suitable for both men and women and are a great deal more comfortable to run in than standard tracksuit bottoms which tend to be of looser fit around the crotch, knee and ankle.

4

The advantage of this type of running leg wear is that they can also be worn when cycling in cooler weather. They are very easy to care for and will wash and dry very quickly. Most good sports shops will stock them, though if you have trouble finding them on the high street you may find your running specialists will need another visit.

Moving up the body there is a variety of clothing that can be worn. In warm weather T-shirts of any design will prove serviceable though there are a number of manufacturers now producing what they call a 'technical' T-shirt. These items are designed to move sweat away from the body and to help you to stay dry throughout your training. This makes them more comfortable and warmer so they can be worn as a summer training shirt and as a winter training base layer. Moving outwards, if the weather is cooler then the best defence is a layered approach with multiple thin layers providing much greater warmth than a single thick layer. This approach also allows a greater degree of flexibility. Sweatshirts and tracksuit tops are suitable, though be careful – some materials may make you sweat or keep the sweat in. This will make all clothing feel damp and if cold will make you feel much colder. There are plenty of specialist items available that can add to your comfort when running but you can spend a lot of money which is not entirely necessary when you probably own some garments that are quite serviceable.

During the colder months of the year gloves and hats can be a useful addition to your running wardrobe. A good quality hat will help retain a great deal of heat during training and is a simple and effective way to stay warm. Gloves generally only need to be thin knitted items though there are, as is always the case, specialist items available. If you are going to be running in the dark or in poor lighting conditions then a high-visibility vest is a very worthwhile investment; these can be picked up very cheaply but again there are some specialist ones available which are designed especially for running.

## SKILLS

Nearly everyone who can walk has the ability to run. It is probably the most natural of all of the three disciplines of the triathlon. Despite this, it is the one that many people find the most challenging. Assuming that you don't have any physical conditions that preclude you from running, such as arthritis, then turning you into a runner is a matter of practice and application. It can be very, very hard work but in health terms it is remarkably simple, you can do it anywhere and the energy expenditure is higher than for the other two disciplines.

Running looks fairly simple but by giving some consideration to the techniques involved we can make it much easier and much more effective for you. Your objective when running is to travel as quickly as possible through the air with as little contact with the ground as possible. Runners have differing techniques, some of which are

90°, relaxed, movement should be forward as well as across the body, and movements should be small, controlled and efficient.

Trunk – Erect, relaxed, hips forwards.

Shoulders – Relaxed, loose.

Foot strike – Under body, either in mid-sole, side of foot or heel. Foot should be pointing forwards.

Take off – Push off quickly after foot strike, heel should come up towards the buttocks.

Stride length – Comfortable and in proportion to the body.

Cadence – Optimum is around 180 strides per minute (90 strides per foot per minute).

more efficient than others. Running styles are governed, to a certain extent, by limb length, body shape and fitness levels. There is a limit to how much a running style can be changed. Improvements are always possible. The basic principle of endurance running is:

Speed = Stride length x Stride frequency

To help you to understand what the basis of a good running technique is, we have listed some general guidelines below:

Head – Should be still with little up and down movement, looking forward.

Arms – Bent at the elbow to approximately

Looking in more detail at running technique, the leg action can be split into a number of phases:

1 The front support phase
2 The drive
3 Recovery
4 Forward swinging

We will expand on each of these areas:

## The front support phase

The objective of this phase is to minimise deceleration at foot strike. With each strike the foot contacts the ground on the part of the foot that is most natural for the athlete. For most athletes the outside of the heel strikes first in longer, slower races and the middle of the forefoot contacts first in shorter, faster races. The support leg cushions the ground contact in a controlled way to minimise braking forces. The arm action is similar to sprinting but is less active or pronounced.

## The drive phase

The objective of this phase is to optimise the forward drive. Your weight rolls over the foot and off the toe of the shoe. Hips, knees and ankle joints extend during this phase; however, in longer distance races this extension may not be complete.

## The recovery phase

The objective of this phase is to contribute to an efficient action and rhythm. This phase begins with the foot breaking contact with the ground, with the trailing leg flexing at the knee and then moving up towards the backside. The heel is brought towards the backside, and the degree of flexion at the knee is dependent on the running speed. This is more pronounced in sprinting activities and less pronounced at slower running speeds.

## The forward swinging phase

The objective of this phase is to prepare for an active foot strike. The recovery leg swings through past the body and upwards but less pronounced than when sprinting. Generally, the slower the speed the lower the knee lift. Once the leg has passed to the front of the body, with the hip flexed, the leg will lower and the knee will extend. The foot then moves down and back relative to the body in preparation to minimise braking at foot strike.

As a general guideline, the body should always be over the lead foot as it strikes the ground. If this is not the case the stride length is too long and the foot striking ahead of the body will apply a breaking force before the body passes over the foot, thus slowing you down. Ideally, the foot plant should be in a straight line in the direction of travel, to ensure that the forces at the take off phase are propelling you forwards. Do not worry if you are displaying other characteristics such as splay footing or pigeon toeing unless this is a clear problem or it is creating injury. If you suspect that this is the case, then you should consult a physiotherapist to correct the fault.

# TECHNIQUE

## Drills to improve technique

Drills are widely referred to in both running and swimming coaching sessions. A drill is simply a specific practice that is used to emphasise and improve a component of technique. It acts by isolating and concentrating on only one aspect of the running action. Many triathlons are won and lost on the run sections of the course – not through lack of stamina, but through an inability to perform an efficient running style. Some basic running drills are listed below which will hopefully improve your running efficiency.

However, different drills are regularly developed, and through spending time working with other coaches you will develop additional drills that can be applied to your sessions. When designing drills you need to consider what aspect of technique it is designed to improve, as well as the technique of actually conducting the drill itself.

When using drills to improve technique you should ensure that you are not fatigued beforehand. Drills should therefore be included at the start of the session after the warm up, when the main aim is to improve technique. Drills should be carried out over a short distance (25–50m) with a walk back to recover. Drills should be repeated between three and six times. When the main component is introduced after the drills, you should keep in mind the purpose of the drills and focus on this during the next component of the session.

Drills can also be very beneficial in acting as a recovery session. This is because they move the limbs through a greater range of motion, thereby helping in the recovery process by maintaining the range of movement and dynamic flexibility. Drills can also be used in the warm-up phase. If doing so, care needs to be taken to make sure that you are fully warm before doing the drill as the drills extend the limbs outside the normal range of motion.

We will include drills during the training programme so keep this section handy for reference.

4

# DEALING WITH INJURY

At this point in the programme it is hoped that you would not have had to deal with injuries. However, they are possible and you are better to be prepared for them than not. There are a number of different types of injury that are not uncommon in sports.

## Falls/collisions

These happen in each of the disciplines but perhaps they are more likely when cycling. There is the potential for a broken bone, but more commonly bruising and damage to the skin. This is best treated by a short rest period for the bruising and cleaning the damaged skin as quickly as possible. There does not need to be a great deal of disturbance to your training programme in this case. If you suspect anything worse than superficial damage then you should probably consult a medical professional. This may require a trip to your local accident and emergency department but if this is the case prepare for a long wait as sporting injuries are, quite rightly, not seen as being high on the list of priorities.

## Overuse

This kind of injury can be difficult to identify. It may start with what feels like a normal ache after a tough training session or training week but if it does not recover in the same way it may be an injury or the beginning of an injury that is developing through overuse. Our programme is designed to reduce the risk of this and therefore the most likely cause is poor technique or incorrect equipment. This is difficult to identify but for swimming re-read the technical sections to look at your stroke, for running make sure your shoes are specific running shoes and of good quality and for cycling make sure the bike fit is appropriate and that the cycling shoe, if used, is set up correctly.

General advice for injuries such as sprains is to rest and ice them. If this is not effective in the first forty-eight hours then consider visiting a doctor for further advice. Regardless of how enthusiastic you are about your chosen race don't risk your long-term health to compete. There are events all over the country and throughout the year so even if an injury forces you out of one before you make it to the start line you will get plenty more opportunities which may not be the case if you cause longer-term damage by continuing with an apparently minor injury.

| DRILL | TECHNIQUE | PURPOSE |
|-------|-----------|---------|
| High knees | Short, very fast steps lifting knees high in front of the body. | Improves running cadence. Improves recovery phase of trail leg. Improves range of motion from the hip. |
| Kick backs | With hands on bottom, kick feet back to touch the hands using a fast action. | Improves running cadence. Improves recovery of trail leg. Improves stride length. |
| Arm drives | As high knees but focus on driving arms through and pumping. | Improves upper body alignment. Improves co-ordination and arm balance. |
| Hills | 15–30 second uphill running on a steepish slope. | Improves stride length. Improves push off. |
| Striding Arm drive Head position | Focus on arm action, all movement driving forwards; focus on keeping head still. | Reduces excess movement. |
| Downhill running | Lean slightly forwards, 'float', avoid braking. | Improves leg cadence. Improves stride length. |
| Long rear legs | Make singular effort to push ground away. Leave foot in contact with ground a fraction longer than normal. | Improves the recovery phase of the cycle. |

You should now have an idea of some of the skills required to train and take part in your triathlon. Triathlon is not an overly complicated sport but there are some specific techniques in each discipline that will make you a more effective athlete and more importantly help you to enjoy your racing more.

Running is accepted as something most people can do but it is often the most challenging for novices. Running for endurance requires determination and a degree of stamina. The physical aspects can be trained for and a sensible approach to running will ensure you reach race day fit and healthy and able to easily cover the distance required.

4

# TRANSITIONING

**As we have identified in the chapters on each individual sport you do have to acquire some specific skills for each element of triathlon. But there is also an important fourth discipline which can be crucial to your success: transition, or the period between the different disciplines.**

Elite level triathletes flow through transition without stopping and are often only in the transition areas for a matter of seconds. Ironman triathletes spend a little longer preparing for the next discipline but even so there is no time wasted. Your objective when moving through the transition area is to prepare for the next part of your race as smoothly and efficiently as possible, completing one discipline and moving on to the next. Speed is important but if your main objective is completion of the event then a brisk transition that ensures you have the right equipment and are within the rules is the most important.

There are two transitions in any triathlon: transition one (or T1) is the transition from swimming to cycling and transition two (T2) is the transition from cycling to running. Elite level triathletes move through transitions at startling speed. For your event you will want to be swift and efficient but you will also want to have a good event and enjoy the day.

5

## SETTING UP TRANSITIONS

You may be allocated a place to set up your equipment or you may have to find yourself a space. You are technically not allowed to mark out your space in transition but make a mental note of where your kit is to help you find it as you dash out of the water or off your bike. There will be a rack on which to place your bike. Hang it by its handlebars or saddle and put your helmet on top of the bike; you must have this on your head and fastened under the chin before you touch or move the bike. Your first priority when leaving the pool will be to get as dry as possible. You may be allowed to take a towel to the poolside and may even be allowed to take some footwear. Often it is just a short distance from the pool to the transition area but there is normally a mat of some sort to run on and the surface you cross will have been prepared by the organisers. If you can't take a towel or footwear put your towel on top of your changing kit: don't worry about getting yourself totally dry as you will be seated during the cycle but get rid of as much of the surface water as you can. Your next step will be the kit you are wearing to ride in: this should be left on top with your shoes underneath. If you are wearing socks make sure you can locate them easily. You may need to put some talcum powder in them to ease them over a wet or damp foot and the same may be the case for your shoes if you are not wearing socks. If you are riding in the same shoes as you are running in then there is little other prep to do for your transition area other

than to make sure that whatever you are wearing has the issued race number secured to it. This number is issued by the race organiser to identify you as a competitor and to help them organise their results. You may need to take some safety pins so you can secure this, as they may not be supplied.

## TRANSITION 1

You are moving from the swim to the cycle section. As you leave the water your body is going from the horizontal to the vertical relatively quickly; couple this with the

towel off and put your shoes on. The distance you have to run to your transition area may vary quite a bit and could be as much as several hundred metres. Once you have arrived in transition your aim is to get out as quickly as possible. Put on your T-shirt, vest or running clothing, ensuring your number is visible and then, before you touch your bike, you must put your helmet on. When you have your helmet on and fastened you can move your bicycle towards the transition area exit. This will be clearly marked as 'Bike Out' or 'Cycle Out'. You must not ride your bike to this point but must push it. You will see a mount line which, as the name suggests, is the first opportunity you have to get on your bike. You must not get on before this line but you should ride as soon as possible after the line and start the cycle section.

adrenalin of a race environment and the excitement generated by spectators and you have what is quite literally a heady combination. Many athletes feel a little dizzy when they first move from the swim to the cycle and if your main objective is completion then it may be worth taking things quite steadily; rather than sprint at full speed from the water, jog gently or walk briskly. Remember you are still racing but it does not necessarily mean you have to go at top speed. You may be able to leave your towel or your shoes on the poolside or near the exit from the pool which, in most cases, is a side door that goes straight outside. If this is not possible you will have to wait until you get to your transition area before you can

## Practices

You will find it a bit tricky to find a pool that will let you either run on the poolside (quite rightly so as it can be dangerous) or head straight outside. So you may find a full practice of Transition 1 a little difficult, but you can practise cycling after the swim. The pause may be a little longer if you take your time passing through the swimming pool changing facilities but some of the sensation will remain. The other really important aspect that can be practised with the minimum of interference to the swimming pool environment is the putting on of your shoes and clothing. Depending on pool rules this may need to be done in the changing rooms rather than at the poolside but it can still be done and the more often it is done, and in the order we describe in this section, the more effective you will be and the faster and more efficient your Transition 1 will be on race day. If you can work a practice of this nature into your swimming training for the rest of the programme you will reap the benefits at the race.

## TRANSITION 2

Transition 2 is the progression from the cycle to the run. It is potentially quite painful but can also be extremely quick. As with Transition 1 there are a number of differences in this transition if you are wearing cycling shoes as obviously these will need to be changed (elite and experienced triathletes who wear cycling shoes can be seen removing their feet from the shoes and pedalling on top of the shoes that are attached to the pedals as they approach the transition line). As with our mounting line there is a dismounting line which is there to show you where you must be off your bike. This is a safety aspect to prevent people from riding inside the transition area and causing accidents. The elite

triathlete will dismount the bike as it moves along, often using the technique that is most commonly seen by postmen and paperboys, who probably get a lot more practice of it than triathletes. If you are wearing cycling shoes this is more difficult than if you are wearing other footwear and involves running on the ground in your bare feet, through the transition area which will have been prepared for this. If you are wearing cycling shoes but don't want to do this kind of dismount then you will need to stop the bike before the dismount line and dismount before entering the transition area either walking or running. If you are wearing your running shoes for the cycle section, Transition 2 becomes a little easier and you can dismount either on the move as we will describe below or you can stop and dismount, always before the line, and then continue into transition as you wish. Your exit out of transition will also be faster as you don't have to change your shoes.

Once you have reached your transition spot, which must be the same one from which you picked up your bike, you can park your bike as required. You must not touch your helmet to undo or remove it until you have placed your bike back on the rack. Once you have racked your bike take your helmet off and then adjust your clothing for the run. This may mean changing shoes. It is unlikely that any other adjustments to equipment will be necessary at this stage.

You can then find the exit from the transition area and set out onto the run course. You may find that running after cycling is a strange and in some cases almost painful experience. Your legs have been used to one action for some time and are now being asked to do something very different. This can be alleviated by lowering your bike gearing for the last few minutes of the ride and then increasing your cadence to maintain your pace. When you set off on the run use a shorter but brisker stride rate to begin with.

## Practices

There are two key areas for practice in Transition 2. The first is the mounting and dismounting of the bike.

As explained above this depends on the type of footwear you select. Make sure that whatever method you choose that you have dismounted by the time you reach the dismount line or you may be penalised by the race officials.

Dismounting on the move is the fastest way of getting off the bike, transferring the bike speed to run speed. If you are using cycling shoes you will need to remove them before you attempt to run as cycling shoes do not grip the ground well and an attempt to dismount on the move while wearing cycling shoes can end in a fall. So either with your feet on top of your cycling shoes or your training shoes on top of pedals, you need to draw one leg up and over the saddle. Then, bring this leg inside and in front of the pedal. You can then, and as you reduce the bike's speed, bring that foot onto the floor, which will lead you into a nice run.

This kind of dismount requires a great deal of practice and you should find a safe area and start at very slow speeds before you progress to an increased pace. It is probably not a good idea to try to do this at the end of a training session when you are tired but schedule it outside training as a specific skill session to give it its own focus.

The other really important part of the second transition that needs practice is the sensation of moving from cycling to running. Regardless of your method of dismounting it is worth working on what we call 'brick' sessions. This is a session that combines both running and cycling and is designed to replicate the transfer from the bike to the run that you will experience during the race. You could either add a very short bike ride to the beginning of a run session or a very short run to the end of the bike session. Both are 'brick' sessions and both will be effective in preparing you for race day.

This fourth discipline of triathlon is what makes the sport unique. The concept of completing each discipline without the watch stopping and the changeover being part of the sport is the aspect that defines the sport. The elite athlete makes this look easy and with a bit of practice you can move through the transition area with few problems and you will look and feel like a triathlete on your race day.

## WHERE AND WHEN TO TRAIN

By this point you will have decided on your event and will have a clear idea of when you need to start training and how long you have until race day. You will have read the section on the equipment you will need to start your training and hopefully organised the basic bits so you can get started. You have also looked at some of the specific skills you will need for the techniques for the three disciplines. We now need to start the training process and take the next step on the road to becoming a triathlete. Before we take this step it is worth considering the support that can be offered by triathlon clubs and clubs that promote the individual disciplines. We have touched on training with others as a great way of staying motivated but the additional support and knowledge that can come from a club is certainly worth considering, particularly if you see triathlon as being part of your life long term. Clubs are not difficult to find and local sports retailers, the ones you have used to buy your specialist kit, will probably be able to help you find your local group.

If you want to train alone or with a partner, we have already covered how to find the time needed to consider the various requirements of your training.

For swimming you obviously need access to a pool. Most pools will state their opening times and many will give an indication of the type of sessions they run. For example many local authority swimming pools are open during weekday mornings but this will probably be shared usage with school groups using the pool for their lessons. This may not create any problems if you don't mind the noise! But swimming lengths may be difficult as the kids are likely to be swimming widths. Equally a Saturday morning session will be dominated by families and leisure swimming and you may not be able to swim unhindered which you will need to do to build up your pace and distance. Checking for the laned swimming sessions or adult-only sessions will give you the best idea of when to go swimming. These sessions are often held early mornings and at lunchtimes with the odd evening thrown in and the times may vary during school holidays so be aware of changing timetables.

You can, of course, cycle on any road at any time of the day or night but finding somewhere to practise and ride that is relatively safe and pleasant is a little more difficult. There are a growing number of traffic-free cycle trails; these provide an environment that is often shared by walkers and occasionally horse riders but is traffic free. They are generally fairly rural though there are a number in major towns and cities. The surface varies from smooth tarmac to a solid trail surface, for which a mountain bike is probably more suitable. Ironically, you may end up driving to these trails so you will need to be able to transport your bike either in or on your vehicle. Once there you can use an out and back route, a route or road that comes back in exactly the same route as you headed out,

reducing the risk of getting lost. It also gives you a really easy way of managing distance and duration which helps you to cycle in a set time. These trails usually have distance markers giving you a clear idea of how far you have been. This is increasingly important as you approach race day as you will want to feel that you can easily cover the cycle distance in the event.

Finding other routes for cycling is simply a question of exploring. If you live in a city this can be more difficult though you may find that there are city parks you can use for cycling around. The countryside gives the best opportunity for you to enjoy your cycling with quieter lanes to explore and outside your training it is this kind of cycling that can be the most enjoyable. When looking for routes to ride consider the volume of traffic, the terrain, the surface and the visibility that the route provides.

You can either use a circular route, which can either be repeated or if required extended as you become more able, or you can use an out and back route that gives you a much easier way of measuring the time and distance you have ridden but can be a little monotonous. Ideally, you need a circular route of half the distance you are going to race with a good safe smooth surface and a couple of small climbs or hills. It should be safe with good visibility throughout and ideally never rained on and always sunny! You may find this type of circuit hard to find but you could just get very fit and proficient at riding your bike just by trying to find it. Finding specific road features to help you practise braking, cornering and climbing will also be useful. A quiet industrial estate will provide you with plenty of corners to practise on; just make sure that they are free from gravel and don't have a loose surface. Finding small hills to practise on should not be too difficult. You need a climb that lasts between two and five minutes to practise your technique and pacing.

The other consideration is time of day. The summer provides plenty of daylight hours with good visibility. From autumn through winter and into spring you need to be aware of the daylight that is available. Having some lights on your bike is always handy in case you do find yourself in failing light, which can come on quickly if the weather changes. Riding and training at night is another consideration altogether and can be a little daunting for the beginner, but it is not recommended.

Your choice of roads needs to be carefully planned, as does your clothing. Generally speaking if you leave your front door feeling slightly cool you will be warm by the time you have been riding for a few minutes. You need to think about basic waterproof clothing, not normally a good idea for leg wear but essential for your upper body, as it can also keep the wind from cooling your body excessively. You will be travelling a little faster than running pace and with your hands exposed so think about gloves. In hot weather you need to ensure you can stay cool and have adequate sun protection. It is not something we would suggest unless you are a very confident rider and have no other opportunity to train.

An alternative to riding at night is to use a static trainer. These are often referred to as 'turbo trainers', which support the bike in a stationary position while allowing you to pedal and provide the resistance against which to work. These trainers are very useful for providing the physical training but they do not give you the opportunity to practise the skills and techniques required to get the feel for the way the bike handles. Therefore, if you are using one during the evenings to fit in your cycle training then you need to try to also ride on the road at the weekends. Any good cycle shop will be able to provide you with a turbo trainer and setting them up is a very simple operation.

The beauty of running is that you can

# THE IRONMAN CHALLENGE

For many people the ultimate triathlon is the Ironman event. It is a specific distance within triathlon and also a specific brand which includes websites, clothing, events and media. There are events all over the world with many countries having only one officially recognised event. Entry to these events is often required many months in advance and is often quite expensive as events on this scale require a great deal of organisation and need many people to make them happen safely. Ironman competition will almost certainly require some travel and accommodation. Most events start very early in the morning to accommodate the length of time it can take some competitors to cover the distances; you may also not feel too inclined to rush off home after completing an event of that degree either. These events need to be planned very carefully and athletes will need to plan months and years in advance to take part in Ironman. Some athletes have entered Ironman as their first event: while this is possible it is probably not advisable but if you decide to take part in one of the big Ironman races you should

follow this book to get you started before increasing your distances, volumes and training intensities accordingly.

Training for an Ironman requires a great deal of commitment with some athletes devoting around twenty hours a week or more to training. This may seem a lot but when you consider the challenge that lies ahead it is not surprising that this volume of training is required. You will find some seasoned triathletes who have tackled the distance as a challenge but are happy to never do it again. There are some athletes who like the distance and compete in Ironman on a regular basis. You will rarely find anyone who does more than two a year, even among the most committed athletes. There is a very small group of elite athletes racing regularly over this distance, while most athletes compete in their age group but more usually are racing against themselves either to complete the event in a time they set for themselves or to beat their previous best time. Either way any athlete who has covered this distance in a competitive environment and has the badge of Ironman competitor deserves a huge amount of respect.

run anywhere at any time, daylight is less of a problem and finding somewhere safe less of a challenge. There are many running tracks around the country owned and run either by clubs or local authorities. They have a good safe surface and it is very easy to measure the distance you have travelled. They do, of course, mean you will need to travel to do your training and this may not be as appealing as simply attacking the pavement outside your home. Running on streets is a common sight, though if you live in a very busy part of a town or city it can be a little more hazardous and involve a lot of dodging. Parks and open spaces provide a more pleasurable experience for running and give you the option of running on grass which can have the benefit of absorbing the shock and impact of the running process. Again choosing a running circuit can help with your motivation as you can easily keep track of the distance you have run. A variety of terrains is also useful but of less importance than for cycling.

## NUTRITION FOR TRAINING AND RACING

Books on sports nutrition cover acres of bookshop space. It can be hugely scientific and very confusing. Couple this with the vast quantity of detailed and often conflicting guidelines given in the media and you can have a very difficult time deciding what you need to do. In the small amount of space available we will give some basic advice to ensure that you have the right fuel in your body to enable you to do the training and then repair afterwards.

Food is fuel – this is a great way to view your food requirements while you train. If you train while hungry it will mean you train less well because you haven't got enough fuel, and it won't help you to lose weight. As a guide, smaller meals throughout the day are much more effective than a larger intake, so avoid having two large meals and instead space out the same amount of food (or possibly less if you are trying to reduce excess weight) into five smaller meals spread through the day. Breakfast is important as it is a kick-start to your day.

There is much talk about a balanced diet but often people do not know what this means. For sport, especially an endurance sport, carbohydrate is probably the most important of the food groups. Carbohydrates are found in breads, potatoes, pasta and rice. When choosing these select the one you like and if possible one that is the wholegrain or 'brown' variety as the health benefits are well documented. Fats are an important part of our diet but are very high in calories for any given volume or weight, and can be damaging as part of an athlete's diet as they can lead to fat being stored by the body. Most people have too much fat in their diet, and by considering the way in which the carbohydrate is served can reduce this amount without any harmful side effects. For example, chips contain more fat than boiled or baked potatoes, so the latter is probably the healthier option. Proteins are also very important for the endurance athlete as they help the body to repair itself. Proteins are found in meat, fish and pulses with the most common of these being baked beans! You should ensure that each meal contains a combination of carbohydrates and protein and also has some fruit or vegetables. A minimum of three meals a day is the key; there is no maximum number of meals you should eat, providing the size is small and the overall quantity not increased unless you find that you are not recovering well and feel lethargic, in which case a fuel shortage may be one of the causes.

Structuring your food intake around your training can be an additional challenge but it will help you train and recover and be as comfortable as possible while you train. You should never train on a full stomach and should leave at least one hour after eating before starting to train. Individually you may need more than this and this will only be established though trial and error; you will also find that different foods take longer to digest than others. You generally are advised to eat relatively quickly after training to help the body refuel. This can be a snack but chocolate, crisps and other sugary and fatty foods are best avoided, regardless of how much your body will be crying out for them. One of the best pre-packaged post training snack foods is the banana, as it contains everything you need and tastes good too. Try not to use food as a reward for training but try to eat to train and train to eat. This will help with weight management and is a much healthier approach to food.

## HYDRATION

Hydration when training is really important. Water is the foundation of all hydration and you should drink before, during and after training. Sipping is the best method before and during but the overall volume in any given day is essential. You should be consuming around three litres a day when resting and possibly double that when training, though it may be even more if the conditions are particularly hot or humid. You can use cordial to flavour your drinks but you should avoid sugary carbonated drinks as they will give you a false feeling of being full and they also slow the hydration process. There are an ever-increasing

6

the weeks leading up the race, not just the day before.

Alcohol is often a part of our lives but it can have a detrimental effect on training. Even relatively small amounts of alcohol will impair your abilities to train, perform and recover, though small amounts of alcoholic drinks are probably better than the feeling of prohibition that can occur if it is seen as banned. Alcohol should never be used for rehydration.

All that is required at this stage and for your event is a sensible approach to nutrition and hydration, and a basic understanding of the demands you are putting on your body.

number of specific sports drinks; some of these are designed specifically as sports fuel, others as recovery drinks. While you may not need the specificity of these products you may find that they help you; the advice of a good sports retailer will be invaluable in finding the correct one for you.

When planning for race day you need to take care that you are adequately fuelled and hydrated but do not feel overfull or bloated. It will take a bit of experimentation to achieve this, which should be done during training. The period running up to the event is also important and you should consider your nutrition and hydration in

# THE IMPORTANCE OF REST AND RECOVERY

The key to a successful training programme is not the training but the rest. It is essential that your body is adequately rested to complete the sessions we have set, and you should consider this when scheduling your week. Four sessions in four days, with three days off, will probably not be as effective as a programme that spreads the sessions throughout the week, making the most of the resting opportunities to allow your body to rest and recover.

It is during this rest and recovery period that your body actually improves and therefore this is arguably the most important section of the training, though obviously how hard you work is a big factor!

A phrase frequently used by sports coaches is 'listen to your body'. This is difficult to describe but refers to your ability to pick up on the relevant signals from the day and decide when you are too tired or not well enough to train. Everyone is different and feeling lethargic and tired after a day in the office may indicate you are too tired to train. However, it may be that training improves the way you feel and leaves you in an invigorated state. Similarly, a stuffy nose and tickly throat may indicate that you have a cold approaching; some people find that some gentle exercise has a beneficial effect on this kind of minor illness while others stop training until they feel 100 per cent better. This is usually based on experience and only time and trial and error will reveal the best strategy for you. The only golden rule is that any symptoms below the neck indicate that training should be suspended until the symptoms are gone. With aches and pains, the approach is similar. As we have discussed you will suffer from aches and pains as you train harder and longer, but this is perfectly normal. Any pain that comes on very suddenly while exercising or is accompanied by swelling should be taken seriously and a doctor should be consulted before you resume training.

Triathlon is a fantastic sport and you have made a great addition to your life by taking one on. You have made great progress to get to this point; all you have to do now is follow the programme and get yourself from the start line to the finish of your event.

Good luck with your programme!

6

# THE 20-WEEK TRAINING PROGRAMME

You have worked through a lot of preparation and you should have everything in place to enable you to start your training. All that remains is the programme itself. The programme will be presented in the following format.

## SAMPLE WEEK

### Session 1 - SWIM
(Session length no more than 45 minutes + changing time)

Two lengths* as fast as you can manage while still being able to complete the total distance set for the session (this will require an element of guesswork but don't start so fast that you can't finish the session).

Rest for 1 minute (use the large pace clock in the pool or count to 100) then go for another 2 lengths again as fast as you can.

Complete this for 4 sets (a total of 8 lengths).

If you have some energy left then practise front crawl technique by swimming 1 length of front crawl counting the number of strokes, and then try to reduce that number during a subsequent length. If you are not a front crawl swimmer practise breast stroke.

### Session 2 - RUN
(Session length 40–45 minutes)

Walk briskly for 10 minutes then jog for 3 minutes.

Drop back to a walk for 2 minutes.

Repeat this 5 times.

Do not worry about the pace and if possible run on grass rather than tarmac.

Once you have completed the session, walk for between 5 and 10 minutes then complete with stretching exercises (see Chapter 1).

### Session 3 - BIKE
(Session length 30–35 minutes)

Using quiet roads or cycle paths find a simple out and back route.

Ride for 15 minutes in one direction.

Pause for 3–5 minutes to take a drink (just water or squash is fine) then ride back.

While riding concentrate on pedalling briskly. Without consciously counting, keep the pedal moving quickly and try to keep pedalling all the time even if going down hill slightly.

Finish the session with stretches.

### Session 4 - RUN
(Session length depending on ability)

This is a test session.

Walk briskly for 10 minutes then run at a steady pace that feels as comfortable as possible for as long as possible.

When you can run no longer, walk for 10 more minutes and complete with stretches.

Make a note of how long you ran for.

* 1 length is assumed to be the standard 25-metre pool length for the purposes of these sessions.

The sessions can be completed in any order and are numbered only to provide some structure. The length of session suggested includes the warm-up and cool-down but does not include the stretching that you will need to do or any changing or travelling time. Do not repeat warm-ups as part of the set where a session states 'repeat x times'. The session includes sufficient detail to guide you through and will give you some opportunity to adapt it to meet your specific needs; there will also be additional hints and tips.

As you progress through the programme do not be tempted to do a great deal more than is prescribed. Always consider the scheduling of your session. We recommend that you run a Monday to Sunday week and therefore, if you swim on Sunday you should probably avoid swimming on Monday.

It is quite likely that you will miss a session in any given week due to the pressures of everyday life. Do not be tempted to try to catch up the following week. This has the danger of creating a great deal of fatigue in any given week which will increase the chances of illness and injury.

The same applies to any week that is missed. It is quite likely that weeks will be missed through illness, injury, holidays or work demands. Providing that the gap does not exceed two weeks this is not going to be a big problem, though if the timing of your event allows resume training at the point at which you left the programme. If the gap is only a week and the event is imminent then this is less of a problem and you should resume at the point you would have been at if you hadn't stopped training.

It is a really good idea to keep a diary as you go through the training programme so you can recall how you felt and how you responded to the training prescribed. If you decide you want to progress further in the sport of triathlon, the information in this diary could prove very useful.

# CASE STUDY PROFILE

## SARAH

You are not the only athlete to take on this challenge.

Our novice triathlete is Sarah. She is a 32-year-old mother of two who works part time as well as running a busy home. She has attended her gym regularly for the past five years (following the birth of her second child) and has tried to go two or three times a week, though this is more an aim than a reality. Sarah feels she would like to be a bit fitter and would like to lose about 2 kilograms to get her back to her pre-pregnancy weight. She feels a triathlon event would be the ideal incentive to keep training and she would like her young children to see her doing something healthy and worthwhile. Sarah has found a local novice triathlon event that she would like to take part in. Following a challenge from a friend she has entered the event. The distance of this event is a 600m swim (normally 24 lengths of a 25m pool), an 18km bike ride (just over 11 miles) and a run of just under 6km (just over 3.5 miles). Sarah does not have a great deal of experience but goes swimming with the children and occasionally on her own. She feels she can swim about four lengths on her own in breast stroke but is not very good at front crawl. Her cycling is often done on an exercise bike in the gym. She has a hybrid bike that she uses when cycling with the children and on holidays. She can ride in the gym for 20 minutes quite easily but says she is not very fast when riding on the road. Her running has been limited to about 10 minutes on the treadmill as part of her gym session. She has not run outside of the gym and is most worried about this section of the triathlon. The event Sarah is taking part in is a swimming pool-based event with the cycle section on the public road and the run around a playing field on grass and pathways.

Sarah will use her normal swimming costume for the swim section in the pool; she will put a T-shirt and close fitting Lycra shorts over this for the bike and run sections. She is planning on using her hybrid bike, but will remove the child seat, lights and luggage rack. She is going to buy a pair of specific running shoes from her local running specialist before she starts running outside the gym. Sarah will follow the programme in this book and we will follow her to race day and track her training progress as she works towards her first triathlon race.

7

# WEEK 1

| SESSION 1 - SWIM | SESSION 2 - RUN | SESSION 3 - BIKE | SESSION 4 - RUN |
|---|---|---|---|
| **Session length no more than 30 minutes + changing time** | **Session length no more then 30 minutes** | **Session length 30–35 minutes** | **Session length dependent on ability** |
| Using the stroke of your choice swim 1 length at a steady pace that feels comfortable (make a note of your time for 1 length). Rest for 30–60 seconds then complete again. This is one set. Complete 8 sets of this; if you can't manage 8 then complete as many as possible. | Walk briskly for 10 minutes then jog for between 30 and 60 seconds. Drop back to a walk for 2 minutes. Repeat this 5 times. Do not worry about the pace and if possible run on grass rather than tarmac. Once you have completed the session walk for between 5 and 10 minutes then complete with stretching exercises. | Using quiet roads or cycle paths find a simple out and back route. Ride for 15 minutes in one direction. Pause for 3–5 minutes to take a drink (just water or squash is fine) then ride back. While riding concentrate on pedalling briskly. Without consciously counting keep the pedal moving quickly and try to keep pedalling all the time even if going down hill slightly. Finish the session with stretches. | This is a test session. Walk briskly for 10 minutes then run at a steady pace that feels as comfortable as possible for as long as possible. When you can run no longer, walk for 10 more minutes and complete with stretches. Make a note of how long you ran for. |

Enjoy this week but don't let the enthusiasm of starting the programme overtake the programme. Sometimes the feeling of wanting to get stuck in can make you feel that you want to do more when, at this stage, it is not necessary. Pace yourself and you will move through the programme easily without too much pain. Use this week to get used to your training equipment and training venues. Learn how your body feels before, during and after training and if required make some notes on how you felt.

# WEEK 2

| SESSION 1 - SWIM | SESSION 2 - RUN | SESSION 3 - BIKE | SESSION 4 - BIKE |
|---|---|---|---|
| **Session length no more than 45 minutes + changing time** | **Session length 40–45 minutes** | **Session length 30–35 minutes** | **Session length about 1 hour** |
| Swim 2 lengths as fast as you can while still being able to complete the total distance set for the session (this will require an element of guesswork but don't start so fast that you can't finish the session).<br><br>Rest for 1 minute (use the large pace clock in the pool or count to 100) then go for another 2 lengths again as fast as you can. Complete this for 4 sets (a total of 8 lengths).<br><br>If you have some energy left then practise front crawl technique by swimming 1 length of front crawl counting the strokes and then try to reduce the number of strokes during a subsequent length. If you are not a front crawl swimmer practise breast stroke. | Walk briskly for 10 minutes then jog for 2. Drop back to a walk for 2 minutes.<br><br>Repeat this 5 times. Don't worry about the pace and if possible run on grass rather than tarmac.<br><br>Once you have completed the session walk for between 5 and 10 minutes then complete with stretching exercises. | Using quiet roads or cycle paths find a simple out and back route.<br><br>Ride for 15 minutes in one direction.<br><br>Pause for 3–5 minutes to take a drink (just water or squash is fine) then ride back.<br><br>While riding concentrate on pedalling briskly. Without consciously counting keep the pedal moving quickly and try to keep pedalling all the time even if going down hill slightly.<br><br>Finish the session with stretches. | Set out to cycle for 1 hour continuously.<br><br>Stop as many times as you feel you need to, but make sure you ride for an hour. |

If you are feeling up to it then you may feel that you want to add a specific bike skills training session. These sessions do not need to be physically demanding and don't need to be very long. Concentrate and practise the skills that you are not very good at, starting with those associated with safety such as starting, stopping and cornering. If you start to feel confident then you can build up to the more advanced skills involved in a quick transition. Make sure these sessions don't become physical training sessions; take it nice and easy and make sure it is about the skills.

# WEEK 3

| SESSION 1 - SWIM | SESSION 2 - RUN | SESSION 3 - BIKE | SESSION 4 - RUN | SESSION 5 - SWIM |
|---|---|---|---|---|
| **Session length no more than 45 minutes + changing time** | **Session length 45–50 minutes** | **Session length 40 minutes** | **Session length 45 minutes** | **Session length variable but no more than 45 minutes** |
| Swim 2 lengths steadily then pause for 1 minute. Aim to complete 5 lengths without stopping at a steady pace. Rest for between 1 and 2 minutes and repeat. Aim to do this 3 times. | Walk briskly for 10 minutes. Jog for 3 minutes then drop back to a walk for 2 minutes. Repeat this 5 times. Don't worry about the pace and if possible run on grass rather than tarmac. Once you have completed the session, walk for between 5 and 10 minutes then complete with stretching exercises. | Using your circuit or out and back route you are aiming for a 40-minute non-stop ride. Don't worry about the pace. | Walk for 10 minutes briskly. Run for 2 minutes. Walk for 30 seconds. Repeat this walk–run set 10 times. Complete 2 of the drills detailed in the skills section and complete a set for 50 metres. Walk back and repeat 3 times each, then walk for 10 minutes to cool down. | Swim 4 lengths to warm up. Swim 1 length as fast as you can then rest for 1 minute. Repeat between 7 and 12 times. |

Three weeks in and you are hopefully starting to become a habitual trainer. At this point exercise and your training sessions will start to become a set part of your life and even in this short period of time your fitness will have started to really improve. Hopefully you now feel comfortable with where you are training and are starting to get to know how you will feel after training. This will help you push harder when the programme requires it.

# CASE STUDY PROFILE

### SARAH AFTER 3 WEEKS

Sarah has found the first three weeks really good fun. Initially she had a few problems setting up the cycle position but spent some time, and a little money, at her local bike shop where the saddle was changed and set at the correct height. Sarah has decided to use her hybrid bike but plans to change the tyres to a lighter, less knobbled type when she gets closer to the race. She has found that the time for cycling has been a bit tricky but is scheduling it into the weekends to help fit it around her work and family commitments. She had an older pair of cycling short passed on by a friend but will probably buy some new ones before the race.

Sarah initially found the pool time a little inflexible but has now found that there are additional sessions that she can attend which are less busy and also a little cheaper. The timing of the sessions has created some scheduling problems but overall has been OK so far.

The running has been a problem. Two sessions were cancelled because of work problems which that meant Sarah was simply not available to do the run or was too tired to start the session. Sarah is trying to find a better way of managing this and plans to have some spare sessions she can use if one gets cancelled. Sarah bought some running shoes after her second session as she developed blisters on her right foot quite quickly. The new shoes are from her local running shop where she also bought some specific sports socks. Now the blisters are OK, the shoes have proven to be worth the investment. The major problem now is just the aches and pains associated with starting a running programme.

Overall Sarah is enjoying her training but finding it tough to fit in. She is sleeping very well.

## WEEK 4

| SESSION 1 - SWIM | SESSION 2 - RUN | SESSION 3 - BIKE | SESSION 4 – RUN | SESSION 5 - BIKE |
|---|---|---|---|---|
| **Session length no more than 45 minutes + changing time** | **Session length 50–55 minutes** | **Session length 45 minutes** | **Session length 55 minutes** | **Session length 75 minutes** |
| Swim 2 lengths steadily then pause for 30 seconds. Aim to complete 5 lengths, without stopping, at a steady pace. Rest for between 1 and 2 minutes and repeat. Aim to do this 3 times. At some point in this session pause to watch a faster swimmer in the pool. Observe how they move through the water and try to emulate this. Try to swim with the minimum of splash. | Walk briskly for 10 minutes then jog for 5. Drop back to a walk for 2 minutes. Repeat this 4 times. If you feel up to it aim to run faster in the last set than the first. Complete 2 of the drills you have not tried, again using a 50-metre straight to do the drill and a walk back. Three times through before your cool down is fine. | Aim for a 45-minute non-stop ride at a steady pace. If you have time do some skills work. | Walk for 10 minutes briskly. Run for 3 minutes. Walk for 20 seconds. Repeat 10 times then cool down with a 10-minute walk. | Ride steadily for 20 minutes. Then, preferably using a slight incline, ride hard and as fast as you can for 3 minutes. Cycle back very steadily for 3–5 minutes and repeat 4 times before resting for 5 minutes followed by a 10–20-minute ride home. |

After a month of training you should be feeling better. If you feel you want to use this programme to change your body shape and lose weight then take some measurements when you first start the programme and then repeat them every month. Use your weight, which should be checked at the same time of the same day of the week. Also measure your chest, arm, upper thigh and stomach; these measurements are a better way of tracking progress than just weight.

# WEEK 5

| SESSION 1 - SWIM | SESSION 2 - RUN | SESSION 3 - BIKE | SESSION 4 - RUN | SESSION 5 - BIKE |
|---|---|---|---|---|
| **Session length no more than 40 minutes + changing time** | **Session length 55–60 minutes** | **Session length 45 minutes** | **Session length 30 minutes** | **Session length 75 minutes** |
| Swim 2 lengths steadily then pause for 1 minute. Aim to complete 10 lengths without stopping at a steady pace. Rest for 1 minute and repeat twice. | Walk briskly for 10 minutes then jog for 6. Drop back to a walk for 2 minutes. Repeat this 4 times. If you feel up to it aim to run faster in the last set than the first. This is the session to add 2 drills; choose ones you enjoy and repeat for 100 metres 3 times with a walk back. Follow this with a steady cool-down and stretch. | Aim for a 45-minute non-stop ride at a steady pace. Add skills practice to this session if you have the time and energy. | Walk for 10 minutes briskly. Run for 10 minutes then walk for 10 minutes. Make sure you cool down and stretch after this session. | Ride steadily for 20 minutes. Then, preferably using a slight incline, ride as hard and as fast as you can for 3 minutes. Cycle back very steadily for 3–5 minutes and repeat 4 times before resting for 5 minutes followed by a 10–20-minute ride home. |

This week may seem like a much tougher week. After the first month you should now be ready to start to increase the intensity of the training. If you start to feel unwell after or during this week then it is perfectly OK to take an extra day's rest.

## WEEK 6

| SESSION 1 - SWIM | SESSION 2 - RUN | SESSION 3 - BIKE | SESSION 4 - RUN | SESSION 5 - BIKE |
|---|---|---|---|---|
| **Session length no more than 40 minutes + changing time** | **Session length 40 minutes** | **Session length 45 minutes** | **Session length 30 minutes** | **Session length 75 minutes** |
| Swim 8 lengths. Pause for up to 5 minutes then swim another 8 lengths. If you feel up to it you can always take this up to a total of 24 lengths as this is the only swim session you have this week. | Walk briskly for 10 minutes then run as hard and as fast as you can for 1 minute. Walk for 1 minute and then repeat 10 times before walking for 10 minutes. It is absolutely vital that you do a good, thorough cool down and stretch after this session as it is quite a tough one. | Aim for a 60-minute non-stop ride at a steady pace. Make the terrain varied and add some skills work if you feel you can. Cornering is a good skill set to add to this session as you can practise at speed. | Walk for 10 minutes briskly. Run for 12 minutes then walk for 10 minutes. This may feel difficult after the previous run session and you should keep an eye on the scheduling and if possible place them a few days apart. | Ride steadily for 20 minutes. Ride as hard and as fast as you can for 2 minutes. Pedal easily for 1 minute and repeat. Use this session to refine the use of the gears. |

The volume and intensity of the training is steadily increasing and you will now be able to feel the training effect in both your training and life outside sport. Take care with your nutrition and general health and hygiene to help prevent picking up colds and sniffles that will impair your ability to train. Hard training can have a detrimental effect on the immune system and it is often a good idea to isolate yourself a little for 15 minutes after training.

# CASE STUDY PROFILE

### SARAH AFTER 7 WEEKS

Six weeks seems to have been a very long time for Sarah. She now feels that the training is fitting in well with her life though there seems to be a weekly problem of some sort or another that gets in the way of one session. Planning an extra spare opportunity has worked in all but one week and has meant she has not really missed any training but in some weeks the sessions have been a bit closely packed which was a little too tiring. She now aches a lot less from the running and is starting to really enjoy the sessions. Her running shoes and socks are combining well and her confidence in the programme overall is increasing.

Swimming has been the discipline to suffer as these sessions are not as flexible and there is often the feeling that the swimming is a rushed experience. The other option which was tried was a session starting at eight in the evening. This was less rushed but Sarah struggled to sleep following the session and felt tired all the following day. This was not repeated.

Sarah feels that she could ride her bike for a lot longer than is set, but finds hills really difficult. She is also not confident in traffic and has spent most time riding around her local parks. She has tried some road sessions but they have been a bit unpleasant. She is having a weekend in the country next week and will try some rural riding whilst away. Sarah has now changed the tyres on her bike and is finding them a big improvement, though this is down to the pressure being set correctly unlike on her old tyres.

## WEEK 7

| SESSION 1 - SWIM | SESSION 2 - RUN | SESSION 3 - BIKE | SESSION 4 - RUN | SESSION 5 - BIKE |
|---|---|---|---|---|
| **Session length no more than 20 minutes + changing time** | **Session length 40 minutes** | **Session length 45 minutes** | **Session length 60 minutes** | **Session length 55 minutes** |
| Swim 12 lengths without stopping. If you feel the need to warm up a bit for this then swim a couple of lengths really gently beforehand. You may also want to repeat this process at the end and also do some stretching. | Walk briskly for 10 minutes then run for 15 minutes without stopping. Walk for 2 minutes then run for another 5. Don't forget to stretch after this session. | Aim for a 60-minute non-stop ride at a steady pace. Distance is more important the pace. | Walk for 10 minutes briskly. Run for 2 minutes then walk for 2. Repeat 10 times then walk for 10 minutes. | Ride steadily for 20 minutes. Ride as hard as you can for 5 minutes then go steadily for 5 minutes. Complete 3 times then pedal home steadily for 10–15 minutes. |

A lot of cycling this week. Hopefully the weather is going to have been kind to you and this will be enjoyable. The fifth session this week on the bike is a tough one and will push you quite hard. This kind of interval training really works and will make you a much faster and efficient cyclist, able to deal with the demands of racing much better.

# WEEK 8

| SESSION 1 - SWIM | SESSION 2 - RUN | SESSION 3 - BIKE | SESSION 4 - RUN |
|---|---|---|---|
| **Session length no more than 40 minutes + changing time** | **Session length 40 minutes** | **Session length 45 minutes** | **Session length 60 minutes** |
| Swim 14 lengths without stopping. As with last week if you want to warm up for 2 lengths and cool down for 2 then go for it; it is not essential but may be useful when working towards your race distance. | Walk briskly for 10 minutes then run for 20 minutes followed by a 10-minute walk. This is your longest non-stop run so far but covering this distance is pretty crucial for your event. | Aim for a 75-minute non-stop ride at a steady pace. Some skills work added to this, either cornering or gear selection, would be good. Your pedalling rate (cadence) should be constant though. | Walk for 10 minutes briskly. Run for 20 minutes followed by a 10-minute walk. After the shorter sessions this week you may find this quite tough but it is certainly going to make you a stronger runner for your race. |

With over 80 minutes of running this week you need to ensure that your technique remains of the highest standard. Refer to the running chapter if required and work on the drills for a little extra time if you feel it is necessary. The stretches are absolutely vital.

**7**

# WEEK 9

| SESSION 1 - SWIM | SESSION 2 - RUN | SESSION 3 - BIKE | SESSION 4 - RUN | SESSION 5 - BIKE |
|---|---|---|---|---|
| **Session length no more than 40 minutes + changing time** | **Session length 40 minutes** | **Session length 45 minutes** | **Session length 60 minutes** | **Session length 55 minutes** |
| Swim 2 lengths to warm up, then swim 4 lengths. Rest for 1 minute and repeat 5 times. This session is about improving your pace so a focus on swimming a little faster during the lengths is the key to the session. Don't forget to cool down and stretch. | Walk briskly for 10 minutes then run for 7.5 minutes. Walk for 2.5 minutes. Repeat 4 times followed by a 10-minute walk. After last week's running we now need to focus a little on running faster so go for it in the 7.5-minute run and use the rest wisely. | Aim for a 90-minute non-stop ride at a steady pace. This will be a fairly long ride and will test your stamina. Despite the fact that you probably won't be riding this long in your race a training ride of this distance will be useful. | Walk for 10 minutes briskly. Run for 2 minutes then walk for 2 minutes. Repeat 12 times then walk for 10 minutes. This session is very much focused on pace. You need to be running quite hard during the run sections. Concentrate on extending your stride length and increasing your stride rate (cadence). | Ride steadily for 20 minutes. Ride as hard as you can for 5 minutes then go steadily for 5 minutes. Complete 3 times then pedal home steadily for 10–15 minutes. |

One of the hardest weeks yet. The volume alone is tough and the content will also leave you knowing that you have trained. The week that follows is easy and should be something to look forward to. This week we train hard; next week we recover and relax a little as you are almost half way through and only 10 weeks from race day.

# WEEK 10

| SESSION 1 - SWIM | SESSION 2 - RUN | SESSION 3 - BIKE |
|---|---|---|
| **Session length no more than 40 minutes + changing time** | **Session length 40 minutes** | **Session length 45 minutes** |
| Swim 12 lengths at a steady pace. As with previous weeks feel free to add a warm up and cool down. This is a slight reduction in distance from our longest sessions but after our speed sessions we should now be able to target a faster swim. | Walk briskly for 10 minutes then run for 15 minutes followed by a 10-minute walk. As with this week's swim session the distance is reduced but we need the pace to be increased a little. | Aim for a 90-minute non-stop ride at a steady pace. As with swimming and running there is more pace this week. |

There are deliberately only three sessions this week. After 10 weeks and half way through the programme it is worth having less strenuous sessions (though the ones that are there are by no means easy) so that you can rest a little and recover. As we discussed in the conditioning section, it is the rest that is important and an easy week is good for morale as well as being effective physically. If you find inactivity a little disturbing then either look at the section that discusses transition practice and work through some of them for the two transition periods in your race, or try to improve your swim technique or some of your cycling skills. Don't feel afraid to do nothing at all and enjoy your rest thoroughly.

# CASE STUDY PROFILE

### SARAH AFTER 10 WEEKS

Sarah has felt well and truly ready for this week and has really enjoyed the fact that there were only three sessions. This has helped her a great deal as she has been feeling a bit sniffly for the past five days before this week but has carried on training to complete the programmes as required. There have been no massive scheduling problems for Sarah in the past month. She has fitted in almost all the sessions, missing only two swim sessions because of problems at her local pool. She did attempt to catch up with these sessions but decided not to after feeling a bit tired.

The weather has helped Sarah with her cycling. She has found that her motivation to get out on the road has improved as the sunlight has increased, and she is really enjoying the road cycling now and feels her skills are improving as well.

Sarah has not yet decided on her race equipment, especially her clothing, but she has been fortunate enough to try on a couple of different styles of racing outfit though she has not yet found one she is entirely comfortable with.

# WEEK 11

| SESSION 1 - SWIM | SESSION 2 - RUN | SESSION 3 - BIKE | SESSION 4 - RUN | SESSION 5 - BIKE |
|---|---|---|---|---|
| **Session length no more than 50 minutes + changing time** | **Session length 40 minutes** | **Session length 45 minutes** | **Session length 60 minutes** | **Session length 55 minutes** |
| Swim 2 lengths to warm up, then swim 6 lengths. Rest for 1 minute and repeat 5 times. | Walk briskly for 10 minutes then run for 10 minutes. Walk for 2 minutes. Repeat 3 times followed by a 10-minute walk. | Aim for a 90-minute non-stop ride at a steady pace. | Walk for 10 minutes briskly. Run for 2 minutes then walk for 2 minutes. Repeat 15 times then walk for 10 minutes. This is a great session to use as a brick session and you can add a short bike ride (10–20 minutes) to the beginning of this session. | Ride steadily for 20 minutes. Ride as hard as you can for 5 minutes then go steadily for 5 minutes. Complete 5 times then pedal home steadily for 10–15 minutes. |

After our easy week last week we are back into it this week with a focus on intervals with all but one session being interval in nature. You should be feeling sufficiently rested in the early part of the week to make the best use of these. It may be worth saving session three until the end of the week when you just want a nice steady session.

7

## WEEK 12

| SESSION 1 - SWIM | SESSION 2 - RUN | SESSION 3 - BIKE | SESSION 4 - RUN | SESSION 5 - SWIM |
|---|---|---|---|---|
| **Session length no more than 30 minutes + changing time** | **Session length 50 minutes** | **Session length 105 minutes** | **Session length 40 minutes** | **Session length 35 minutes** |
| Swim 20 lengths. This is a good session to practise your transition drills. | Walk briskly for 10 minutes then run for 10 minutes. Walk for 2 minutes. Repeat 3 times followed by a 10-minute walk. A good session to add the short bike at the start and give you transition practice. | Aim for a 105-minute non-stop ride at a steady pace. This is a long session but a short (10–15 minute) run could still be added to the end if you feel up to it. | Walk for 10 minutes, run for 20 minutes, walk for ten minutes. | Swim 2 lengths steadily. Swim 3 lengths as hard as you can. Rest for 2 minutes then repeat 6 times. |

Quite a long bike ride for session three this week. In all disciplines we are aiming to be able to go beyond the distance set for the event so you can have every confidence in yourself on race day. This kind of training is great for burning some fat and getting your muscles used to endurance. Two swim sessions this week also provide a bit of a push in the pool and these will probably be quite tough sessions.

# WEEK 13

| SESSION 1 - SWIM | SESSION 2 - RUN | SESSION 3 - BIKE | SESSION 4 - RUN | SESSION 5 - BIKE |
|---|---|---|---|---|
| **Session length no more than 30 minutes + changing time**<br><br>Swim 8 lengths. Rest for 90 seconds. Repeat 3 times. | **Session length 50 minutes**<br><br>Walk briskly for 10 minutes then run for 8 minutes.<br>Walk for 2 minutes.<br>Repeat 4 times followed by a 10-minute walk. | **Session length 75 minutes**<br><br>Aim for a 75-minute non-stop ride at a steady pace | **Session length 40 minutes**<br><br>Walk for 10 minutes.<br>Run for 25 minutes.<br>Walk for 10 minutes. | **Session length 40 minutes**<br><br>Ride at a pace slightly faster than normal for 40 minutes. |

Almost three quarters of the way through the programme and you should be feeling fitter and faster and should be comfortable with your training and competency at the individual disciplines. With only a few weeks to go think carefully about the equipment you are planning to use and order any kit you haven't got that you will need. It is also probably worth looking at your travel and accommodation plans if these are required for your chosen event.

7

## WEEK 14

| SESSION 1 - SWIM | SESSION 2 - RUN | SESSION 3 - BIKE | SESSION 4 - SWIM | SESSION 5 - BIKE |
|---|---|---|---|---|
| **Session length no more than 30 minutes + changing time** | **Session length 50 minutes** | **Session length 75 minutes** | **Session length 40 minutes** | **Session length 40 minutes** |
| Swim 8 lengths. Rest for 90 seconds. Repeat 3 times. Add a transition practice to this session if possible. | Walk briskly for 10 minutes then run for 8 minutes. Walk for 2 minutes. Repeat 4 times followed by a 10-minute walk. | Aim for a 75-minute non-stop ride at a steady pace. Add a run transition practice to this session. | Swim 20 lengths non stop. | Ride at a pace slightly faster than normal for 45 minutes. |

The run session this week is probably the tough one, though it can often feel that there are no really easy sessions. Being out on a run for this length of time, combined with the intervals, will prove a real challenge but it will make you a stronger runner and better triathlete in the long run.

# WEEK 15

| SESSION 1 - SWIM | SESSION 2 - RUN | SESSION 3 - BIKE | SESSION 4 - RUN | SESSION 5 - SWIM |
|---|---|---|---|---|
| **Session length no more than 30 minutes + changing time** | **Session length 50 minutes** | **Session length 75 minutes** | **Session length 40 minutes** | **Session length 60 minutes** |
| Swim 10 lengths. Rest for 90 seconds. Repeat 3 times. Add a transition practice if possible. | Walk briskly for 10 minutes. Run for 10 minutes. Walk for 2 minutes. Repeat 4 times followed by a 10-minute walk. | Aim for a 75-minute non-stop ride at a steady pace. Add a transition practice to this session if possible. | Walk for 10 minutes. Run for 25 minutes. Walk for 10 minutes | Swim for 2 minutes steadily. Rest for 30 seconds. Swim as hard as possible for 4 lengths. Rest for 1 minutes. Repeat 8 times. |

Next week we have our second really easy week and to get the most out of it we need to go into it a little fatigued. Four interval sessions and one long bike session will ensure you feel sufficiently tired by the end of the week and the recovery process will build stronger, more athletic muscles.

# CASE STUDY PROFILE

### SARAH AFTER 15 WEEKS

The increase in the intensity and volume over the past few weeks has proved very challenging for Sarah and initially this dented her confidence a bit as she felt that she had progressed but was then finding the training as difficult as it had ever been. This created a motivational problem for a week around week 12 but after feeling really tired Sarah started finding the training a little easier for a week or so, and responded to the programme well. Her improved fitness and differing rate of progression proves that not everyone responds to training in the same way.

Sarah has missed a number of sessions due to a very difficult project at work which required some extra time working at home. This also caused Sarah to doubt herself but weeks 13 and 14 have given her a great deal of confidence and some great sessions on the bike and with the run have really boosted the way she feels about the training.

Sarah's close friends now know she is doing the race and are planning to watch. This has created some extra pressure but Sarah is keen for the day to be one to remember.

# WEEK 16

| SESSION 1 - SWIM | SESSION 2 - RUN | SESSION 3 - BIKE |
|---|---|---|
| **Session length no more than 30 minutes + changing time** | **Session length 40 minutes** | **Session length 90 minutes** |
| Swim 30 lengths non-stop. | Run for 40 minutes non-stop. | Ride for 90 minutes. |

This is a much easier week than previous weeks. This is deliberate; you have had a period of intense training and now need to take an easier week to ensure you don't become over trained or fatigued.

## WEEK 17

| SESSION 1 - SWIM | SESSION 2 - RUN | SESSION 3 - BIKE | SESSION 4 - RUN | SESSION 5 - SWIM |
|---|---|---|---|---|
| **Session length no more than 30 minutes + changing time** | **Session length 50 minutes** | **Session length 75 minutes** | **Session length 40 minutes** | **Session length 60 minutes** |
| Swim 12 lengths as fast as you can whilst still being able to complete the set distances. Rest for 90 seconds. Repeat 3 times. | Walk briskly for 10 minutes then run for 10 minutes. Walk for 1 minute. Repeat 4 times followed by a 10-minute walk. | Aim for a 75-minute non-stop ride at a steady pace. | Walk for 10 minutes. Run for 25 minutes. Walk for 10 minutes. | Swim for 2 minutes steadily. Rest for 30 seconds. Swim as hard as possible for 5 lengths. Rest for 1 minute. Repeat 8 times. |

We are starting to get really close to race day and you need to start thinking about how it is going to feel. This will help you tackle the nerves that you will inevitably feel at the event. Some basic mental rehearsal and picturing of how the race will go for you will help. It is basic sports psychology but it is effective.

# WEEK 18

| SESSION 1 - SWIM | SESSION 2 - RUN | SESSION 3 - BIKE | SESSION 4 - RUN | SESSION 5 - SWIM |
|---|---|---|---|---|
| **Session length no more than 30 minutes + changing time** | **Session length 50 minutes** | **Session length 75 minutes** | **Session length 40 minutes** | **Session length 60 minutes** |
| Swim 35 lengths at a steady pace. | Walk briskly for 10 minutes. Run for 35 minutes. | Aim for a 75-minute non-stop ride at a steady pace. | Walk for 10 minutes. Run for 5 minutes Walk for 1 minute. Repeat 8 times. Walk for 10 minutes. | Swim for 2 minutes steadily. Rest for 30 seconds. Swim as hard as possible for 5 lengths. Rest for 1 minute. Repeat 8 times. |

This is a good steady week which you are now more than capable of dealing with. There is nothing in here to push you too hard but it may feel a little tricky as you will be starting to fatigue before we rest before the event.

7

135

# CASE STUDY PROFILE

### SARAH AFTER 18 WEEKS

Sarah knows the race is getting very close. She has planned her transport and is having her bike serviced at the beginning of next week. She has finally sorted out her race clothing and will be wearing a one-piece trisuit with a T-shirt over the top for the bike and the run. She had her first sports massage from her friend last week and this really helped. Her kit is in place, she knows she has done the training and now is really getting excited about her race.

# WEEK 19

| SESSION 1 - SWIM | SESSION 2 - RUN | SESSION 3 - BIKE | SESSION 4 - RUN | SESSION 5 - BIKE |
|---|---|---|---|---|
| **Session length no more than 30 minutes + changing time**<br><br>Swim 10 lengths at a good fast pace.<br>Rest for 2 minutes.<br>Repeat 4 times. | **Session length 50 minutes**<br><br>Walk briskly for 10 minutes.<br>Run for 20 minutes at a good pace.<br>Walk for 2 minutes and repeat twice followed by a 10-minute walk. | **Session length 75 minutes**<br><br>Aim for a 75-minute non-stop ride at a steady pace. | **Session length 40 minutes**<br><br>Walk for 10 minutes.<br>Run for 5 minutes<br>Walk for 1 minute.<br>Repeat 8 times.<br>Walk for 10 minutes. | **Session length 120 minutes**<br><br>Ride steadily for 10–20 minutes.<br>Ride as hard as you can, preferably on a hill or incline for 5 minutes.<br>Ride steadily for 2–3 minutes.<br>Repeat 8 times then ride home for 10–20 minutes. |

Next week is the final week. It will be an easy one after this week which was effectively your last week of proper training. Make sure all your race preparations are in place and start looking forward to your race.

7

## WEEK 20

| SESSION 1 - SWIM | SESSION 2 - RUN | SESSION 3 - BIKE |
|---|---|---|
| **Session length no more than 30 minutes + changing time** | **Session length 30 minutes** | **Session length 75 minutes** |
| Swim 25 lengths steadily. | Run for 30 minutes. | Aim for a 75-minute non-stop ride at a steady pace. |

Enjoy your race!

# CASE STUDY PROFILE

### SARAH'S RACE

'A great day was had by all' always sounds like a bit of a cliché. Sarah and her family and friends enjoyed the event. Sarah woke early with nerves and did some early preparations which enabled her to feel really calm as her allotted start time approached. Her swim went very well but Transition 1 was very difficult for Sarah and despite practice she felt very dizzy and a little sick in the early part of the transition and ended up walking when she had planned to run. The bike was good and with great weather Sarah enjoyed it though it was a little windy on the way back to the transition, making it a little slower than she would have hoped. Sarah ran a lot faster than she expected but was able to hold the pace for the duration of the run and came in with a really good time. Sarah felt really energised by the process of the race but slept like a log.

Sarah is now keen to go longer and faster and has enquired at her local club about training with them.

## POST-RACE

You will have crossed the line in, let's hope, a euphoric state, having achieved the goal that you have spent a great deal of time working towards. For some people this can lead to a bit of an empty feeling once the initial joy has worn off. You need to enjoy your moment and make sure you tell everyone about your achievement. You will almost certainly get a medal and probably a race T-shirt to commemorate your achievement and you will probably receive notification in the week following the event of your official race time, position overall and age group position. Keep this information for both reference and possible future use. You are now a triathlete.

You may have taken up this challenge to get a bit fitter, to lose weight, to win a bet or to raise money for charity. Regardless of your motivation you have achieved something that is worthwhile and something that you should be proud of. You have improved your overall health and fitness, and learned new skills. So, what should you do with this now?

Well, you could return to your 'old' life and leave the training as a distant memory but that seems a shame given all the hard work you have put into your training to get this far. Or you could progress in the sport of triathlon. There are many ways in which you can progress and the direction you take is going to depend on your overall motivation and what you enjoy. In this book we have mentioned duathlon and aquathlon, these are both triathlon derivatives that appeal to different athletes. The very strong swimmer who dislikes cycling will favour the aquathlon; while the runner who can ride a bike well but does not like getting wet can progress in duathlon. There is obviously the challenge of going faster and it may be that you take your race time and try to beat it at the same event next year or your may decide to try another event over the same distance that will provide you with the challenge of increasing your pace. As we started with a sprint distance triathlon there is the obvious progression of increasing your race distance. You may target the long distance events such as Ironman or you may move up to the standard distance or Olympic distance events that are very common for age group championship competition throughout the world. Whatever you decide, your grounding through this book will have set you on the right path.

Congratulations and good luck!

# APPENDIX A: THE RULES

All sports have their rules – while you may not need to memorise all the minute details, it is worth having a good understanding of the competition rules so you don't inadvertently transgress them as you may be penalised and this would have a very detrimental effect on your day.

## GENERAL RULES

- Competitors must exercise sound, mature judgement, carry out all reasonable instructions from officials, obey the laws of the land and observe traffic regulations.
- Competitors must follow instructions given by the police. Failure to do so will result in disqualification and may lead to disciplinary action by British Triathlon.
- Competitors are ultimately responsible for their own safety and for the safety of others.
- Competitors must take responsibility for knowing the rules and abiding by them.
- It is the competitor's responsibility to be properly prepared for an event and to ensure that their equipment is suitable and fit for its intended purpose.
- It is the competitor's responsibility to know and correctly complete the full course of the event.
- Triathlon, duathlon and aquathlon are individual endurance events. Any teamwork that provides unfair advantage over other competitors is expressly forbidden.
- No competitor shall be permitted to continue racing who, in the opinion of any race official, is physically incapable of continuing without sustaining physical damage or loss of life.
- It is recommended that British Triathlon members do not participate in triathlon, duathlon and aquathlon events that have not been registered with British Triathlon. British Triathlon insurance does not cover the member while participating in such an event, which may not meet the safety standards of British Triathlon. Participation may also render the member ineligible for selection to a National team. For the purpose of these rules this applies to Age Group, Junior, U23 and Elite teams.

## RACE CONDUCT

- Competitors must conduct themselves in a proper manner and not bring the sport into disrepute.
- All other competitors, officials, volunteers and spectators must be treated with respect and courtesy.
- Threatening, abusive or insulting words or conduct are not permitted and competitors may be disqualified for using such.
- All competitors must wear any official swim cap, bib or numbers provided by the race

organiser. These must be worn unaltered and be both visible and/or readable at all times (see Race numbers).

- Competitors must be adequately clothed at all times, the minimum being a one- or two-piece non-transparent swim suit together with a cycling or running top if appropriate. All competitors must ensure that their upper body (especially the chest area) is clothed during the cycling and running sections of the event.
- Race equipment must not be discarded at any point on the course but must be placed in the athlete's allotted position in transition; see Penalties.
- No individual support by vehicle, bicycle or on foot is permitted except as provided by the organisers. Competitors may not receive any assistance other than that provided by the race organisers.
- Parents/guardians/accompanying adults: failure by a parent/guardian/accompanying adult to carry out instructions from officials, or failure to conduct themselves in a proper manner may lead to disqualification of the competitor and/or disciplinary action against the competitor by British Triathlon. Misconduct by a parent/guardian/accompanying adult may include, but is not limited to:
  - threatening, abusive or insulting words or conduct
  - failure to obey marshals'/officials' instructions
  - handing water bottles or any other equipment to, or collecting them from, competitors
  - tampering with the equipment of others
  - unsporting impedance.

# TRANSITION AREAS

- In order to avoid accidents, safeguard equipment and protect personal possessions, athletes must not bring helpers, friends or family members into any transition area.
- Pets are not permitted in the transition area.
- Equipment must be PLACED in its allotted position and not where it may hinder the progress of other competitors. Equipment that is discarded will be regarded as a hindrance and a time penalty may be issued; see Penalties.
- Cycles must be placed in their correct allotted position both at the start and finish of the cycle section. Cycles should be racked by either the seat pin or by the handlebars/brake levers unless other arrangements are provided. Cycles which are incorrectly racked may be determined as being an impedance to other athletes; see Penalties.
- Competitors must mount their cycles and start riding only when the parts of both wheels which touch the ground are outside the transition area (i.e. at or beyond the officially designated cycle start).
- When returning to transition competitors must dismount their cycle before any part of the cycle leaves the 3m dismount zone, which should be clearly marked before the end of the cycle course. They may then walk or run with their bike to its allocated position.
- Competitors must not interfere with another competitor's equipment in the transition area.
- Competitors must not use any device to mark their position in transition. Any device

or marker will be removed by the referee but if this is not possible a penalty will be applied; see Penalties.

# RACE NUMBERS

- Race numbers provided by the organiser must not be altered, cut down, folded or in any way mutilated. Numbers so treated will result in a time penalty to the competitor if the offence is not corrected.
- Race numbers must be affixed to the competitor's clothing or to a suitable race belt or bib so that the number is clearly visible at all times.
- During the cycling phase a number must be displayed to the rear.
- During the running phase a number must be displayed to the front.
- Additional body marking may be provided by the organiser but this is not a substitute for, or replacement of, an official race number.

# SWIM CONDUCT

- Competitors may stand, or rest on the bottom, or on a non-moving object, but may not gain unfair advantage or make progress, other than is deemed necessary to execute entry into and exit from the designated swimming course by doing so. In shallow waters, an exact point when swimming must commence and may cease shall be appointed and marked.
- Competitors shall at all times swim so that they do not deliberately obstruct or interfere with other competitors. Making contact other than by accident shall be declared unsporting impedance.
- Race organisers may set a time limit for the swimming section. The time limit will be determined when the event is registered with British Triathlon and be published in all race information and must be covered in all race briefings.
- At the end of the specified time limit any competitor still in the water shall be ordered to retire. Competitors refusing to retire will not be insured to continue racing and may be subject to disciplinary action by British Triathlon.
- At all events, both pool-based and open water, no diving is permitted unless pre-agreed at the time of registering and then only for entry at the start of the swim and for re-entry on multiple lap courses.

# CYCLE CONDUCT

- Every competitor must ensure that his or her cycle is in a safe and roadworthy condition and conforms to the technical specifications laid down by British Triathlon.
- During the event, competitors are individually responsible for the repair of their machines.
- Where a competitor is preceded or followed for any length of time, or frequently passed, by the same motor vehicle not provided by the organisers, that vehicle shall be considered as being associated with the competitor and to be giving support.
- Any part of the cycle course may be covered on foot but on these occasions the competitors must carry or push their own machines.

- All competitors must follow the normal rules of the road, obey all traffic signals and follow any instructions given by the police. Any infringement of the law and subsequent legal action is the sole responsibility of the competitor.
- Competitors shall at all times cycle so that they do not deliberately obstruct or interfere with other competitors. Making contact other than by accident shall be declared unsporting impedance.
- Helmets must be fastened before the competitor's cycle is moved from its allotted place in the transition area and must remain fastened until the cycle is returned to this position at the end of the cycle section of the race. Failure to do so may result in a time penalty; see Penalties.

# PACING/DRAFTING

- Competitors are not allowed to draft, i.e. take shelter behind or beside another competitor or motor vehicle during the cycling segment of races.

## Bicycle draft zone

For all age group events (except long distance):

The draft zone is a rectangle measuring seven (7) metres long by three (3) metres wide which surrounds every cycle on the cycle course. The front edge of the front wheel defines the centre of the leading three- (3) metre edge of the rectangle. A competitor may enter the draft zone of another competitor but must be seen to be progressing through that zone. A maximum of 15 seconds is allowed to progress through the draft zone of another competitor. If an overtaking manoeuvre is not completed within 15 seconds, the overtaking cyclist must drop back.

For all competitors in long distance competitions (elite and age group):

The draft zone is a rectangle measuring ten (10) metres long by three (3) metres wide which surrounds every cycle on the cycle course. The front edge of the front wheel defines the centre of the leading three- (3) metre edge of the rectangle. A competitor may enter the draft zone of another competitor but must be seen to be progressing through that zone. A maximum of 30 seconds is allowed to progress through the draft zone of another competitor. If an overtaking manoeuvre is not completed within 30 seconds the overtaking cyclist must drop back.

- The draft zone of one competitor may not overlap the draft zone of another competitor.
- Competitors may enter the draft zone of another competitor for the purpose of overtaking as detailed above or in the following circumstances:
    - For safety reasons.
    - At an aid station.
    - At the exit or entrance of a transition area.
    - At an acute turn, such as a 180° turn around a traffic cone.
    - If race officials exclude a section of the course from the drafting rule because of narrow lanes, construction, detours or for other safety reasons.

When a competitor is passed by other competitors, it is his/her responsibility to move out of the draft zone of the overtaking competitor. A competitor is passed when another competitor's front wheel is ahead of his/hers.

Side-by-side riding, while still observing the draft zone, is only allowed on courses that are fully closed to other traffic. On open or semi-open courses, only single-file riding is allowed.

## Vehicle draft zone

Competitors are not allowed to gain unfair advantage by drafting on officials' escort vehicles, TV and radio vehicles, etc. The vehicle draft zone is a rectangle thirty-five (35) metres long by five (5) metres wide which surrounds every vehicle on the cycle course. The front edge of the vehicle defines the centre of the leading five-metre edge of the rectangle. The driver of the vehicle, who must be appropriately briefed by the organiser, is responsible for upholding the zone.

## Draft legal events

In events where there are draft legal waves British Triathlon will follow the current ITU ruling on drafting. This may require equipment such as aero bars to be changed (visit www.triathlon.org to view current ITU rules).

# RUNNING CONDUCT

- No form of locomotion other than running or walking is permitted.
- Competitors shall, at all times, run so that they do not deliberately obstruct or interfere with other competitors. Making contact other than by accident shall be declared unsporting impedance.

# PENALTIES

- Competitors may only be penalised by readily identifiable race referees.
- All infringements are to be reported to the senior race referee who will have the responsibility of posting penalties.
- Penalties may be issued or disqualifications given at any time up to the announcement of the final results, except where drug testing is involved, when results must be considered provisional until test results are known.

The following penalties will be imposed for infringements.

## Disqualification

a. Threatening, abusive or insulting words or conduct
b. Breaking road traffic regulations
c. Dangerous conduct/riding
d. Diving (but see Swim conduct)
e. Failing to obey marshals or the police
f. Nudity
g. Outside assistance
h. Tampering with the equipment of others

i. Unsporting impedance – including but not limited to incorrectly racked bikes, discarded equipment and the use of marking devices which impede others

j. Two (2) drafting violations noted by motorcycle referee(s) OR four (4) reports from static draft-control marshals OR one (1) drafting violation noted by a motorcycle referee and three (3) reports from static draft-control marshals. NB: there is no requirement for a draft-control marshal to indicate that a competitor has been reported

k. Course irregularities (unless the competitor returns to the point at which he/she left the course, or a point on the course prior to it, and then completes the course)

l. Breach of conduct by parent/guardian/accompanying adult

**Disqualification if fault not rectified after a warning**

m. Illegal equipment (swim, cycle or run equipment)

n. Banned equipment including, but not limited to, mobile telephones, MP3 players and personal stereos

o. Illegal progress (during swim, cycle or run)

p. Racing topless

**Two-Minute Penalty**

q. Helmet violations (unclipping helmet whilst in contact with the cycle)

r. Number violations (not able to be altered after a warning)

s. Riding in the transition area

t. Markers in transition that cannot be removed but do not impede the progress of others

u. Drafting: One (1) drafting violation noted by a motorcycle referee OR three (3) reports from static draft-control marshals. NB: there is no requirement for the marshal to indicate that a report has been made.

**Notes:**

- In the interests of safety, motorcycle referees will NOT provide an audible or visible warning for a drafting violation.
- The race referee may issue a discretionary two-minute penalty for infringements not listed above.
- Penalties will be posted as soon as they are available, on the penalty board, by the senior referee. The penalty board will be provided by the race organiser and placed at an agreed position with easy access for competitors e.g. near transition or next to the results display.
- In the case of any athlete or their parent/guardian/supporter(s) using threatening, abusive or insulting conduct, British Triathlon will consider disciplinary action against that athlete.

# APPENDIX B: GLOSSARY

Below is a list of the terms you will find used in the triathlon world:

**Aerobic fitness**: The ability of an individual to undertake activity while using oxygen as a fuel.

**Age group**: The way in which the majority of non elite athletes compete. Five year age bands from the age of 20 up to 80+. This allows all athletes to be champions within their own age groups and also to represent their country at European and world championships.

**Anaerobic**: The ability of an individual to undertake intensive activity at a level at which the body is no longer using oxygen as a fuel.

**Aquathlon**: An event comprising a swim followed directly by a run.

**Bilateral breathing**: The ability of a swimmer to breathe to both the right and the left.

**Bottom bracket**: The section at the bottom of the bicycle where the chain-ring and cranks are joined through the frame. A point that requires great rigidity.

**Cadence**: The speed at which you complete a given action, used most commonly in cycling and referred to the number of times the pedals revolve in a minute (revolutions per minute or RPM). Also used in running to refer to the amount of times the foot hits the floor in a minute and also in swimming for the number of strokes performed in a minute.

**Chain-ring**: The large sprocket attached to the pedals in the centre of the bike. Usually there will be two or possibly three chain-rings attached to the pedals by cranks.

**Clipless pedals**: Pedals that attach to the bottom of the shoes usually using a mechanism of springs.

**Conditioning**: The physical state of readiness for any given individual.

**Drafting**: The practice of gaining an advantage by racing behind somebody else. Most effective in cycling and within five metres of the rider in front though there is also a benefit in the swim and run. There are rules preventing this in the majority of triathlon. See also non drafting.

**Drills**: The practice of repeating a small portion of a skill often in an exaggerated form to enhance the ability of an athlete in performing the skill in race conditions.

**Dry tri**: An event comprising three events based in a gym, usually a set distance on a rowing machine followed by a set distance on a static bike and then on a treadmill.

**Duathlon**: An event comprising a run followed directly by a cycle followed by a final run.

**Elite (athlete)**: An athlete who is considered to be among the best in the country. There is no official measure of elite but it is a title generally accepted by peers.

**Endurance**: The ability to sustain a given workload for a long period.

**Fitness:** A very wide term used to describe an athlete's state of readiness. See also conditioning.

**Flexibility**: The ability of an athlete to move a limb around the joint in the full range of movement.

**Gears**: The collection of sprockets that are used on bicycles to vary the resistance and speed of progress. There will be a gear mechanism at the back and probably also at the front near the chain-ring.

**Headset**: The section where handlebars and stem meet the frame of your bicycle and swivel.

**Hydration**: The liquids you drink. A well-hydrated individual would have consumed sufficient appropriate liquids to sustain life and activity at an optimum level.

**Intensity**: The level at which you undertake a given action or exercise is referred to as the intensity. Working very hard would be an intensive workout, while working out very gently would be a low-intensity workout.

**Interval training**: The practice of using small intervals of time within a training session where the training is extremely hard. This is to replicate the demands of racing in small chunks to help the athlete improve.

**Ironman**: A long distance race of a 2.4-mile ocean swim, 112-mile bike race and 26.2-mile run; also a registered trade name.

**Lactate threshold**: The highest intensity at which the body can function before the production of lactic acid exceeds the ability of the body to reprocess it.

**Lactate tolerance**: As an athlete becomes fitter he or she can operate at a greater intensity before reaching the lactate threshold. This is the point at which the body is producing more lactic acid in the muscles than it is removing and re-synthesising.

**Lactic acid**: The waste product from the muscles when the body operates anaerobically.

**Mass start**: An event in which a large number of people start at once rather than at set intervals such as every minute. All competitors may start at once or they may be in groups, often referred to as waves.

**National governing body**: Each sport has a body which represents the interests of that sport in that country. Within Britain it is the British Triathlon Association and above this there is the European and international triathlon unions. To compete at national championship level or above you must be a member of your national governing body.

**Non drafting**: An event where drafting is not allowed.

**Nutrition**: The food you eat.

**Open water**: A piece of water such as a lake, reservoir, sea or river that is used for swimming. An outdoor pool would not be considered to be open water.

**Periodisation**: The practice of planning a training programme over a long period such as a year and assigning different periods different titles and objectives.

**Race belt**: A belt worn with the sole purpose of displaying a race number so that it can be moved from the front during a run and to the back during the cycle section.

**Saddle height**: The height measured from the top of the pedal axles to the top of the saddle. Not to be confused with frame height.

**Sprint**: A flat out effort at top speed.

**Sprint distance**: A race that is much shorter in distance. Strictly speaking it is a race of half the distance of the standard distance but often the distances are much shorter.

**Standard distance**: Often referred to as Olympic distance as it is this race distance that is competed over in the Olympic games. The race is 1500m swim, 40km bike and 10km run.

**Static trainer**: Often referred to as a turbo trainer. Normally an A frame that holds the back wheel of a bicycle whilst applying a roller to the back wheel of the bicycle for resistance.

**Strength**: Can describe either maximal strength, which is the ability of an individual to complete a given workload in very short amounts, for example lifting a very large weight once; or muscular strength and endurance, which is the ability of an individual to sustain a workload for an extended period.

**Transition**: The area in triathlon where your equipment will be stored and you will enter and exit between disciplines.

**Trisuit**: A specially made suit of one or two pieces and used for the duration of a triathlon.

**Wet suit**: A suit used for swimming made from neoprene. The suit is designed to trap a layer of water between the body and the suit which is then warmed by the body.

# Bike map

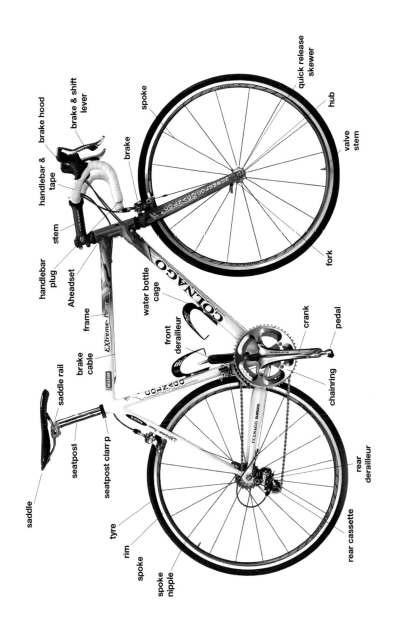

- brake & shift lever
- brake hood
- handlebar & tape
- spoke
- quick release skewer
- hub
- valve stem
- brake
- stem
- handlebar plug
- Aheadset
- fork
- frame
- water bottle cage
- front derailleur
- crank
- pedal
- brake cable
- saddle rail
- chainring
- seatpost
- seatpost clamp
- rear derailleur
- saddle
- tyre
- rim
- rear cassette
- spoke
- spoke nipple

# APPENDIX C:
# USEFUL WEBSITES

There is a mine of information regarding triathlons to be found on the internet, but the following websites are good starting-points.

www.britishtriathlon.org
www.triathlon.org
www.usatriathlon.org
www.220magazine.com
www.triathlonireland.com
www.triathlonwales.org.uk
www.triathlon.org.au
www.triathloncanada.com
www.insidetri.com
www.triathlon.org.nz
www.ironman.com

# INDEX